AF785984

MIX
Papier aus verantwortungsvollen Quellen
Paper from responsible sources
FSC® C105338

Telaye Fikadu Mulubiran

An assessment of Woreda Capactiy

The case of Gindeberet and Abuna Gindeberet Wereda in Oromia National Regional State

Anchor Academic
Publishing

Mulubiran, Telaye Fikadu: An assessment of Woreda Capactiy: The case of Gindeberet and Abuna Gindeberet Wereda in Oromia National Regional State. Hamburg, Anchor Academic Publishing 2013

Buch-ISBN: 978-3-95489-182-5
PDF-eBook-ISBN: 978-3-95489-682-0
Druck/Herstellung: Anchor Academic Publishing, Hamburg, 2013

Bibliografische Information der Deutschen Nationalbibliothek:
Die Deutsche Nationalbibliothek verzeichnet diese Publikation in der Deutschen Nationalbibliografie; detaillierte bibliografische Daten sind im Internet über http://dnb.d-nb.de abrufbar.

Bibliographical Information of the German National Library:
The German National Library lists this publication in the German National Bibliography. Detailed bibliographic data can be found at: http://dnb.d-nb.de

All rights reserved. This publication may not be reproduced, stored in a retrieval system or transmitted, in any form or by any means, electronic, mechanical, photocopying, recording or otherwise, without the prior permission of the publishers.

Das Werk einschließlich aller seiner Teile ist urheberrechtlich geschützt. Jede Verwertung außerhalb der Grenzen des Urheberrechtsgesetzes ist ohne Zustimmung des Verlages unzulässig und strafbar. Dies gilt insbesondere für Vervielfältigungen, Übersetzungen, Mikroverfilmungen und die Einspeicherung und Bearbeitung in elektronischen Systemen.

Die Wiedergabe von Gebrauchsnamen, Handelsnamen, Warenbezeichnungen usw. in diesem Werk berechtigt auch ohne besondere Kennzeichnung nicht zu der Annahme, dass solche Namen im Sinne der Warenzeichen- und Markenschutz-Gesetzgebung als frei zu betrachten wären und daher von jedermann benutzt werden dürften.

Die Informationen in diesem Werk wurden mit Sorgfalt erarbeitet. Dennoch können Fehler nicht vollständig ausgeschlossen werden und die Diplomica Verlag GmbH, die Autoren oder Übersetzer übernehmen keine juristische Verantwortung oder irgendeine Haftung für evtl. verbliebene fehlerhafte Angaben und deren Folgen.

Alle Rechte vorbehalten

© Anchor Academic Publishing, Imprint der Diplomica Verlag GmbH
Hermannstal 119k, 22119 Hamburg
http://www.diplomica-verlag.de, Hamburg 2013
Printed in Germany

Dedication

This thesis is dedicated with heartfelt love and devotion to my mother W/ro Hamelmal Wasie who sacrificed her golden times and happiness in life to see her son where he is now.

Acknowledgement

First and for most I would like to thank my advisor Professor C.D.Dash for his academic guidance and constructive criticism in the course of the study. Furthermore, my gratitude also extends to my parents especially to my mother Hamelmal Wasie who have played a great role in shaping and making my life bright.

Furthermore, I owe my deepest gratitude to my uncle Ato Fetene Getachew and his wife W/ro Getenesh Gosaye for their parental love they showed and thought me. My heartfelt thanks also goes to my younger brothers Abel Fetene and Kidanemariam Fikadu, and my elder brother Kinde Wasie for their brotherly advice and moral throughout the program.

Moreover, I woul like to extend my gratitude to my father Ato Fikadu Mulubrihan; and W/ro Mihret for their advice, moral and financial support throughout the program.

Besides, my appreciation goes to public servants of Gindeberet and Abuna Gindeberet Weredas who thought me a lesson about the challenges of real research. Moreover, I would like to extend my gratitude to the study Wereda officials who participated on the focus group discussion and key informants for their valuable information they provided me. Above all, I would like to extend my heartfelt thanks to Gindeberet Wereda TVET administration and Abuna-Gindeberet Wereda Finance and Economic Development office administration for allowing me their premise to organize the focus group discussion.

Further, my gratitude also extends to my aunt Tewabech Belay, my brothers Nebro Kefyalew, Eshetu Mulubiran, Alemu Beza, Belay Dagnachew, my uncles Dagnachew Hunegnaw and Teferi Alemu, and my friends Fufa Abetu, and Abera Benti who have highly engaged in the collection of questionnaires.

Finally, I also thank all those who have contributed in one-way or another to the successful completion of my study but whom I do not have mentioned their name.

Table of Contents

List of Abbreviations

ACBF- African Capacity Building Foundation

BPR-Business Process Reengineering

BSC- Balanced Score Card

CBDSD- Capacity Building for Decentralized Service Delivery

CBOs-Community Based Organizations

CHIP- Civil Society Human and Institutional Development Program

DLDP-District Level Decentralization Program

ICT-Information Communication Technology

NCBP-National Capacity Building Program

NGOs-Non-Governmental Organizations

OECD- Organization for Economic Cooperation and Development

PS-Professional Science

PSCAP-Public Sector Capacity Building Program

SDPRP-Sustainable Development and Poverty Reduction Program

SPSS-Statistical Package for Social Science

SWOT- Strength, Weakness, Opportunity and Threats

TVET-Technique Vocational Education and Training

UN-United Nations

UNCRD- United Nations Center for Regional Development

UNDP- United Nations Development Program

WB-World Bank

WGLL- Peace Building Working Group Commission on Lesson Learned

LIST OF TABLES

Title **Pages**

Abstract

This research assesses woreda capacity in Gindeberet and Abuna Gindeberet Woreda of West Shoa Zone Oromia National Regional State since the implementation of District Level Decentralization Program. To this end, the research has assessed the human resource, financial, managerial, facility capacity as well as the extent to which enabling work environment and community participation is available. In order to achieve these objectives, qualitative and quantitative research approaches were used. Furthermore, to generate qualitative and quantitative data primary and secondary sources were employed. Key informant interview, questionnaires, and focus group discussions were used as primary sources whereas financial and human resource reports and other relevant documents were used as secondary sources. Both probability and non-probability sampling techniques were employed.

The finding of the study indicated that the capacity building program which was launched to address the problem of rural woredas has not brought about significant changes or could not bring about the desired change though there are some improvements in terms of community participation, service delivery and responsiveness to customers. It has also empowered woreda civil servants to provide decisions on their own. However, constraints of resources and its utilization, lack of conducive work condition, lack of strong political leadership and commitment, and lack of governance system have been identified as factors responsible for the ineffectiveness of the program. Accordingly, the study found out among other things, problem of adequate and competent human resources as well as lack of managerial capacity. Furthermore, woredas have limited financial and human resource autonomy as well as lack autonomy to set priority and targets. Besides, low revenue generating capacity has forced woredas to heavily rely on block grant from the regional government. Moreover, the overall work environment was not conducive and attractive as inter alia organizational structures were unclear, unstable and complex as well as there was weak coordination and communication among local governance actors. The level of the participation of the community in matters affecting their life was found not to the desired level.

It is therefore, generally recommended that for the capacity building effort to be materialized and achieve the desired objectives, there is a need to fulfill the following conditions that enhances the successful implementation of the program, viz. availability of resources and proper utilization, strong political leadership and commitment, enabling work environment and the governance system has to be improved.

Chapter One

1 Introduction

1.1 Background of the Study

Decentralization and local governance are not a new concept though their emergence and exposure to academic discourses and discussions is a recent phenomenon. The two concepts are highly interrelated and interdependent concepts as local governance is defined to be the interaction between or among different local governance actors (private, public, and civil society organizations) as well as the coordination and integration among different sectors; whereas decentralization is a process that involves the transfer of planning, management, resource raising and allocation responsibility and functions from the central government and its agencies to one or more of the following local governance actors or institutions: field units of central government ministries or agencies, subordinate units or levels of government, semiautonomous public authorities or corporations, area-wide, regional or functional authorities, or nongovernmental private or voluntary organization.

Accompanied by one or more of the following benefits of decentralized governance like improving the life of people at local level, enhancing human development, and deepening democracy, bringing the government closer to the people, promoting government responsiveness and accountability, increasing government's flexibility to address diverse needs of the population, reducing corruption through enhanced oversight, promoting the dispersal of power from monopolized political structures, and ensuring allocative efficiency (Rondinelli, et.al., 1983; Smoke, 2003; Rondinelli, 1999; Rondinelli, et.al, 1989; Litvack, et.al., 1998; Devas, 2006; Olowu, 2001; Conyers, 2006; Shah and Thompson, 2004; Hadingham, 2003; Lister and Betley, 1999; Cheema and Rondinelli, 2007; Crawford and Hartmann, 2008; Faguet, 1997; Middleton et.al., 1987) though the result is one of mixed (Rondinelli, et.al., 1983), several countries have embraced one or more forms of decentralization as a means to promote participatory development and governance.

Ethiopia has a limited experience of decentralization compared with several other African countries in which developed system of local government prevailed from colonial powers legacy.

The effort to decentralize responsibility and power was begun in the country during the reign of emperor Menilik II with the purpose to ease the tension between the center and the periphery on the one hand and the administrative systems on the other (Daniel, 1994). The effort continued under the reign of emperor Haileselassie I who issued different proclamations and decrees such as the administrative decentralization of 1942, and Order No. 43 of 1966 to empower *awrajas* with a deconcentrated responsibility and functions and promote rural development as well as bring the growing local government activities in to manageable dimensions (Tegegne and Kassahun, 2004; Meheret, 2002; Dickovick and Tegegne, 2010; Fenta, 1998). The Derg regime also continued the top-down system of administration through establishing a centralized and unitary state. Furthermore, the regime had instituted Urban Dwellers Associations and Peasant Associations and Service Cooperatives as an instrument to bring about economic, political and social development through devolving substantial authority (Yigremew, 2001). However, decentralization with the objective of empowering citizens and devolving power was not exercised and genuine.

In order to realize the benefits of decentralization the present government has adopted decentralized system of governance through the 1995 constitution that declared the country as federal government comprising of nine national regional states and two administrative cities (Addis Ababa and Dire Dawa) with power and authority to self-rule. The constitution has empowered regional governments to have their own legislative, executive and judicial power; to pass legislation on matters falling under their jurisdiction, to enact state constitution and other laws consistent with the federal constitution; formulate and execute economic, social and development policies, strategies and plans; administer land and other natural resources as per the federal laws; levy and collect taxes and duties on revenue sources reserved to them and to allocate and administer budget; enact and apply laws on the state civil service and their condition of work; and establish and administer state police force, and maintain public order and peace within their jurisdictions (Federal Democratic Republic of Ethiopia, Constitution, 1995, Article 50 & 52).

Even though, Article 50 (4) of the federal constitution proclaimed that in order to enable the people participate directly in the administration of local units adequate power to be granted to the lowest units of government, in the 1990s the initiative of decentralization was mostly limited to regional level without clear definitions of powers and duties of the lower tiers of government. It is only from 2001 onwards that Ethiopia began to adopt a decentralized form of local governance characterized by devolution.

As a result, the 2001 revised constitution of Oromia National Regional State has established woredas as one of the basic tiers of government for the provision of services as they are closer to the grassroots population. Accordingly, the region's constitution Article 76-89 has empowered woredas *inter alia* to plan, approve, implement and evaluate social services, economic development and public administration, oversee the activities of basic agricultural development and natural resources, mobilize and activate the community for development, ensure the proper collection of land use taxes, agricultural income taxes and other taxes as determined by the law, and utilize revenues that falls within its jurisdictions.

Furthermore, the government has launched nationwide capacity building initiatives to be headed by the Ministry of Capacity Building. Accordingly, the National Capacity Building Program (NCBP) with an emphasis to 14 sectors was launched among which District Level Decentralization Program was inaugurated mainly to address local capacity challenges in rural woreda areas (Dickovick and Tegegne, 2010; MoFED, 2002).

1.2 Statement of the Problem

Ethiopia has been ruled by a highly centralized system of governments which did not allowed local autonomy and local discretion to lower tiers of government. Accordingly, local governments under the previous two regimes served as a field agent and instrument of control over local population.

However, the 1991 governmental change has ushered in a decentralized system of governance in which power was devolved from the center to regions to enable different ethnic groups develop their culture and language, manage socio-economic development in their respective jurisdictions, exercise self-rule and bring about an equitable share of national resources among the regions, promote harmony among different groups and develop self-rule (Meheret, 2002; Tegegne and Kassahun, 2004; Tegegne, 2007). Moreover, the practice of decentralization in Ethiopia was a response to the hitherto highly centralized system of governance on the one hand and the federation created under the previous unitary system on the other (Assefa, 2006).

The realization of effective decentralization relies on the presence of certain conditions such as the availability of resources like human resources; financial resources; and physical infrastructures and how best they are utilized; the willingness and the commitment of leaders at different levels; the presence of conducive organizational conditions; the attitude of the local people towards the government and the commitment of local leaders; and appropriate institutional capacity (Rondinelli, et.al., 1983; Rondinelli, et.al, 1989). However, in Ethiopia these conditions were hardly available as the decentralization policy, particularly of Woredas, were characterized by administrative and institutional capacity gaps, viz. shortage of administrative and personnel capacity to carry out socio-economic functions and poor revenue base, lack of independent taxation authority and restrictions on raising local revenue have inhibited effective self-government, lack of adequate decision making power and self-rule, and compelled them to heavily rely on support from regional and central governments (Meheret, 2002; Tegegne and Kassahun, 2004; Dickovick and Tegegne, 2010, Yegremew, 2001).

Realizing these facts the government has launched National Capacity Building Program that comprises of 14 sectors, (such as civil service reform, tax reform, justice reform, district decentralization, information and communication technology, private sector, construction sector, urban management, cooperatives, textile and garments, agricultural training of vocational and technical levels, industrial training of vocational and technical levels, civil society, and higher education) which involves a systematic combination of human resources, working systems and institutions that would enable a country to achieve its development objectives. Furthermore, in collaboration with the World Bank the government has initiated a five-year Capacity Building for Decentralized Service Delivery Project (CBDSD) with the objective to improve service delivery performance by building public sector capacity at the federal, regional, and local levels of the country's decentralized government system (Yegremew, et.al, 2005; Dickovick and Tegegne, 2010; MoFED, 2002).

Furthermore, in order to alleviate the capacity gaps of local governments District Level Decentralization Program was designed to deepen democratization process, enable legislations, fiscal reform, institutional restructuring, and to establish more offices to be manned through redeploying employees from regional and zonal administrations (MoFED, 2002).

However, there are little evidences that show the extent to which the capacity building program was effective in filling the capacity gaps that have already been identified. Furthermore, there were no priorly undertaken studies to assess the result of capacity building initiatives in the two study woredas. Hence, this is the gap that this study wishes to fill with a particular focus on Gindeberet and Abuna Gindeberet Woredas in Oromia National Regional State.

1.3 Objectives of the Study

1.3.1 General Objectives of the Study

The general objective of the study is to examine whether capacity building program's process is effective in bringing about the desired outcomes in Gindeberet and Abuna-Gindeberet woredas with focus on variables like human resources, financial capacity, enabling environment, community participation and other related issues.

1.3.2 Specific Objectives of the Study

In accordance with the stated general objective, the study has addressed the following specific objectives:

- Describe the basic constitutional functions assigned to woredas under study.
- Analyze the overall activity of the two woredas in the area of human resource development (training and development) to enhance the performance of local government employees.
- Assess human resource capacities of woredas under study in terms of adequacy, qualifications, and skills.
- Assess the availability of the necessary infrastructures and office equipment to the successful implementations of local development plans and functions.
- Identify the financial capacity of the woredas under study.
- Assess the existing enabling work environments (both internal and external enabling environments).
- The extent of community participation in local development planning, implementations, monitoring and evaluation.

1.4 Research Questions

The study has addressed the following basic research questions:

- What are the basic functions and responsibilities assigned to woredas under study?
- Do woredas (Gindeberet and Abuna-Gindeberet) have adequate, qualified and skilled Personnel?
- Do woredas have adequate fiscal capacity and resources to undertake local development planning, monitoring and executions?
- Do woredas have adequate infrastructure and office equipment's to run local socio-economic development?
- Is the environment (internal and external) conducive to effectively execute local functions and responsibilities?
- To what extent local government under study engage the local community in matters that affect their life?

1.5 Research Design and Methodology

In order to capitalize on the strength of both approaches and compensate for the weakness of each approach the research has made use of the combinations of qualitative and quantitative research approaches. Qualitative approach particularly case study is selected as it represents a comprehensive and in-depth observation, description, explanation, analysis of many components of a given social situations or analysis of individual case that be a person, group, episode, process, community, society, a program, event, activity, process, or one or more individuals or any other unit of social life with the purpose to develop as full understanding of that case as possible. It aims to understand the case in depth, and in its natural setting, recognizing its complexity and context. Moreover, case study places more emphasize on the full analysis of a limited number of events or conditions and their interrelations (Babbie, 1973; Kumar, 1999; Creswell, 2009; Punch, 1998; Kothari, 2004).

Thus, case study is justified so as to enable a thorough investigation of the case through exploring attitudes, behavior and experiences by using such research techniques like interview, focus group discussions, and unstructured and semi-structured questionnaires. It is also preferred due to the fact that the research involves empirical inquiries and assists to collect as many data as possible about the subject under study etc.

Two cases are selected in order to maximize the data and reach at a stronger conclusion about the issue under study.

On the other side of the coin, quantitative research approaches descriptive survey method is employed as it produces quantitative information about the social world and describe feature of the characteristics of large population, and analyze several variables simultaneously (Babbie, 1986; Neuman, 1994). It helps to reach on generalized proposition about human behavior, attitudes, beliefs/opinions, characteristics, expectations, self-classifications, knowledge, etc. It helps to get the greatest amount of understanding from the fewest number of variables, provides empirical verifications and it is logical (Babbie, 1973; Neuman, 1994). It is also used to explain or explore. Moreover, it is probably the best method to collect original data for describing population too large to observe directly, and it is excellent tools for measuring attitudes and orientations in a large population (Babbie, 1986). Besides, it saves time and costs.

Descriptive survey research is important for the study as it has a paramount importance to analyze several variables, provide empirical justification, and to collect original data. Moreover, it helps to measure the attitudes and beliefs of large sample in relatively short period of time. Besides, survey research is desirable as the research comprises of tabulation and statistical treatment. Furthermore, descriptive survey research is preferable as the main target of the research is to assess how effective capacity building is in the two study woredas and how adequate the resources available are. Moreover, it has paramount importance as the researcher has investigated the capacity building challenges and opportunities of the two woredas under study.

1.5.1 Sample Size and Selection

Woreda level administration is taken as a focal point due to the fact that they are key local units of government as they play key roles in prioritizing the provision of public services (Loop, 2002). The two woredas are selected due to the convenience the researcher has in terms of access to collect data. Moreover, they are also selected to compare the two woredas as Gindeberet is the forefather of Abuna-Gindeberet woreda. Last but not least, Gindeberet and Abuna Gindeberet woredas are selected due to the fact that they are considered as remote area though they are only about 180 and 184KM respectively from Addis Ababa.

The study has made use of both probability and non-probability sampling techniques. A probability sampling is proved if a sample is representative of the population from which it is selected and if all members of the population have equal chance of being selected in the sample (Babbie, 1973). Accordingly, in order to provide all civil servants of both woredas equal chance of being selected and avoid bias, simple random sampling was employed. Accordingly, the names of the woreda civil servants were found and samples were drawn using the 'lottery' method of selection.

Moreover, the non-probability sampling used was purposive and convenience sampling. According to Neuman (1994), purposive Sampling is appropriate in three situations; to select unique cases that are especially informative; to select members of a difficult-to-reach, specialized population; to identify particular type of cases for in-depth investigation. Having this factors in mind key interview informants and focus group discussion participants' were selected purposively based on their familiarity to the issue, their seniority, as well as the different positions they held at different time so that it enables to get more reliable and dependable information about the issue under study. In spite of its disadvantage, convenience sampling is used in order to address questionnaires to members of woreda cabinets and councils as it is difficult to administer the questionnaires to all of them since most of their members are not on job and in session respectively.

Survey sample must represent the populations from which they are drawn if they are to provide useful estimates about the characteristics of that population (Babbie, 1973). Accordingly, Gay (1981), points out that the minimum number of subjects believed to be acceptable for a study depends upon the type of the research work involved. For descriptive survey research, a sample of 10% of the population is considered minimum; for a smaller population 20% may be required. Therefore, for the sake of this study 20% is considered as reasonable in order to attain the objectives of the research. Accordingly, in Gindeberet and Abuna Gindeberet woreda official document's showed the presence of 544 and 314 employee respectively out of which 20% of sample size is drawn. Accordingly, the sample size for Gindeberet and Abuna Gindeberet woreda is about N=108 and N= 63 respectively. Furthermore, questionnaires concerning the issue of finance was distributed to N=11 and N=7 officials who are both members of cabinets and woreda councils of Gindeberet and Abuna Gindeberet woreda as they were on training and are not in a session respectively.

1.5.2 Data Collection Techniques

For the purpose of this research both primary and secondary sources of data were utilized in order to generate qualitative and quantitative data's. Qualitative data's were collected from primary sources of data such as interviews, questionnaires, focus group discussion and personal observations. Secondary sources of data such as official reports and publications, working papers, national and regional constitutions as well as other laws are reviewed in order to prepare the socio-economic and demographic profile of both woredas, and to understand the formal responsibilities and functions of woredas under study as different from other tiers of government. In addition, books, journals, electronic materials and other publications were also reviewed.

Furthermore, quantitative data are generated by making use of both primary and secondary sources of data. Primary data are collected through questionnaires administered to samples selected from civil servants, members of woreda councils and cabinets while the remaining quantitative data's are gathered from secondary sources such as survey statistical reports and organizational documents.

1.5.2.1 Questionnaires

In order to able to generate both qualitative and quantitative data that provides comparable results and obtain in-depth information questionnaires that have 7 parts were prepared in English language and translated to Afan Oromifa due to the widespread use of the later language and all were administered to both woreda sectoral civil servants except the parts that deals with finances which was distributed to woreda officials (members of cabinets and councils). Accordingly, all questionnaires were returned effectively.

1.5.2.2 Focus Group Discussion

The hall mark of focus group is the explicit use of the group interaction to produce data and insights that would be less accessible without the interaction found in a group (Morgan cited in Punch, 1998).

Lunt and Livingstone cited in Flick (2002), stated that the general strength of focus group is twofold: it generates discussions, and so reveal both the meaning that people read into discussion topic and how they negotiate those meanings. Second, it generates diversity and differences, either within or between groups, so reveals the dilemmatic nature of every day arguments.

Thus, focus group discussion was conducted in order to clarify and counter check the information or data collected during key informant interviews as well as through questionnaires. Furthermore it was undertaken to better understand and cross check the present situation. According to Flick (2002), it is more appropriate to organize focus group discussion with strangers instead of groups of friends or of people who know each other very well, because the level of things taken for granted which remains implicit tend to be higher in the latter. Hence, to clarify the data collected and to get the general perception of the respondents two focus group discussions, having 12 and 8 participants are invited from different woreda sector offices which have actual experience with the issue of capacity building program and other senior civil servants who have worked at different positions in Gindeberet and Abuna Gindeberet woreda respectively, were organized towards the end of the fieldwork.

1.5.2.3 Interview with Key Informants

Interview is useful when participants cannot be directly observed, allows researcher control over the line of questioning, to attain higher response rates, to guard against confusing questionnaires items, it is the most flexible method, and helps to get answer to all questions (Creswell, 2009; Babbie, 1973; Neuman, 1994; Kumar, 1999; Kothari, 2004). Moreover, it is very good way of accessing people's perceptions, meanings, definitions of situations and constructions of reality as well as understanding individual or group perspectives (Punch, 1998).

In descriptive survey studies, structured interview is quite often useful technique because of its being more economical, providing a safe basis for generalization and requiring relatively lesser skill on the part of the interviewer (Kothari, 2004; Kumar, 1999). Hence, in order to collect dependable and reliable information about the issue under study and to counter check the response collected through questionnaires, interview with key informants that the researcher thought are more informed about the study were conducted. Accordingly, Head of woreda Civil Service and Good Governance office, Deputy Head of woreda Civil Service and Good Governance office and Coordinator of Work Process, Human resource Management Core process owner, and previous Head of capacity building office of each woreda were interviewed by using semi-structured questionnaires.

In addition, in order to gather an in-depth information and valuable data unstructured interview was undertaken as unstructured interview is characterized by flexibility of approach to questioning capable of producing rich and valuable data. It is important in a situation whereby either in-depth information is needed or little is known about the area (Kumar, 1999; Kothari, 2004).

1.5.2.4 Document Analysis

Creswell (2009) states that document analysis enables a researcher to obtain the language and words of participants, unobtrusive sources of information, as written evidence saves a researcher the time and expense of transcribing. In light of this, different official documents (budget proclamation and human resource report as well as documents showing the profiles of the woredas were used as in put to the study.

1.5.3 Data Analysis and Presentation

Once the necessary data's and information are at hand, both quantitative and qualitative methods of data analysis were employed. In this regard, for quantitative data's gathered through questionnaires a descriptive statistical analysis was used. To this end, tabulations, and Statistical Package for Social Science version 17 (SPSS) were employed to describe the data at hand. Moreover, qualitative methods of analysis were used to analyze information gathered from official documents, interviews, focus group discussions and questionnaires.

1.6 Significance of the Study

The second wave of decentralization which aimed at strengthening the capacity of woredas was launched in 2001. It aimed at enabling legislations for local governments, fiscal reform, institutional restructuring, capacity development, etc. Moreover, it has devolved more power and responsibilities to district level administration.

Therefore, it seems important that such moves and others are backed by research efforts as the country has very minimal experiences of decentralization as compared to centuries of centralized governance the country has undergone. In light of this, the study has paramount importance to:

- Woredas under study by showing their capacity gaps and issues that deserve attention for future solution.
- Generate valuable information about the capacity of woredas as they are the key units of local governance in Ethiopia.
- Helps higher authorities and policy makers to take measures to overcome woredas capacity constraints.
- Encourage future research.

1.7 Scope and Limitations of the Study

The national government of Ethiopia has launched capacity building initiatives under National Capacity Building Program with District Level Decentralization Program focusing on rural local government levels. Accordingly, in making assessment of whether this government effort has achieved the intended objective at woreda level, the study has focused on selected variables that help measure capacity of local governments such as human resources, financial capacity, enabling environment, community participation and other related issues (woredas).

Moreover, given the time, budget, transportation service, topographic features and other constraints, the study was confined to employee that are currently working at sectoral offices of the two woredas (Gindeberet and Abuna-Gindeberet). Hence, civil servants and other employee who were currently working at kebele level were not part of the study.

There are also information constraints to fully assess the performance of capacity building program given data collection and analysis are poorly developed at woreda level. Furthermore, since capacity building is an ongoing process it is difficult to get or collect all sorts of information and make a comprehensive and conclusive generalization.

2. Organization of the Paper

The study will consist of four main chapters. Accordingly, chapter one mainly introduces the study, problem statement, objectives of the study, and research design and methodology of the study. Chapter two set the framework of the study and reviews relevant literatures on the subject. The main part of the paper, analysis of the collected data, is presented in chapter three of the study. The last chapter will make concluding remarks and forward possible recommendations.

Chapter Two

Review of Literature

2.1 The Concept of Capacity

The literature devoted to capacity is abundant and covers a wide range of disciplines, from economics to education, from management to public policy. Each discipline gives different meanings to the term depending on the users and the context in which the term is used. Accordingly, some authors define capacity as the ability of doing something or the ability to perform (CHIP, 2007; Walters, 2007; Baser and Morgan, 2008; Horton, 2002). Accordingly, capacity is the proven ability of key actors in a society to achieve socio-economic goals on their own that is demonstrated through the functional presence of a combination of viable institutions and respective organizations; commitment and vision of leadership; financial and material resources; skilled human resources (Farrell, 2007). According to this definition capacity is the ability of individuals, organizations and societies to perform functions, solve problems, and set and achieve goals as well as design, implement, manage, monitor and evaluate development policies and programs in order to achieve the intended goals and objectives successfully (UNDP, 2006; Baser and Morgan, 2008; Browne, 2002; Fukuda-Parr, et.al., 2002; Koning, et. al., 2006; ACBF, 2011; OECD, 2006; Leautier, 2010). Capacity is therefore the product of deeply embedded processes connected to both societal and individual abilities and motivations to manage their overall affairs successfully.

Capacity is the emergent combination of attributes, assets, capabilities and relationships that enable a human system to perform, survive and self-renew (Baser and Morgan, 2008; Ubels, et.al., 2010). This definition makes clear that capacity is not a static state or quality. It is about creating some form of added value for the members and the outside world (perform), it is about staying alive and active (sustain), it is about adjusting and developing over time (self-renew) on the basis of external pressures and internal drivers.

Capacity is about ability to identify challenges and constraints and react to these situations. Accordingly, Gbla and Rugumamu (2003), states that capacity is the ability of organizations, organizational units, individuals and societies to identify constraints and to plan and manage development effectively, efficiently and sustainably. This definition involves both the development of human resources, institutions, society and a supportive policy environment. It encompasses the process by which individuals, groups' organizations and societies develop their abilities individually and collectively, identify their problems and constraints to development, set development objectives, formulate policies and programs, perform functions required to solve the identified problems and achieve a set of development objectives.

Capacity is the ability of an organization to function as a resilient, strategic and autonomous entity (Baser and Morgan, 2008; Kaplan, 2000). This entails that capacity represents the potential for using resources effectively, mastering change and the adopting of new ideas, and maintaining gains in performance with gradually reduced levels of external support (Fowler and Ubels, 2010). It is the broader ability of a system to live an active and meaningful life and demonstrate confidence in determining its own future. Capacity is inherently relational that involves interaction with its environment, influencing and being influenced. In this regard, Brinkerhoff (2010), argues that capacity is the aptitudes, resources, relationships and facilitating conditions necessary to act effectively to achieve some intended purpose.

Moreover, Lavergne and Saxby (2001), argue that capacity highlights the ability of individuals, organizations or society as a whole to do several things: to be guided by key values and a sense of purpose, to define and analyze their environment and their own place in the greater scheme of things, to define the issues and reach working agreements on purposes or mandates, to manage and resolve conflicts, to formulate strategies, to plan, and act on those plans, to acquire and mobilize resources, to learn new skills and approaches on a continuous basis, to build supporting relationships with other parties, to assess performance and make adjustments, to meet new challenges proactively, by adjusting agendas, approaches and strategies.

Generally, Baser and Morgan (2008) characterize capacity as:

- **Empowerment and identity** - Capacity has to do with people acting together to take control over their own lives in some fashion.
- **Collective ability,** The combination of attributes that enables a system to perform, deliver value, establish relationships and to renew itself.
- **A state or condition which is inherently a systems phenomenon.** Capacity involves a complex combination of attitudes, resources, strategies and skills, both tangible and intangible.
- **A potential state.** It is elusive and transient. Capacity is dependent to a large degree of intangibles. It is thus hard to induce, manage and measure. As a state or condition, it can disappear quickly particularly in smaller, more vulnerable structures.
- **The creations of public value.** All countries, regardless of their level of development, have effective capacity that subverts the public interest.

While specific wording and emphasis may differ, there is a general consensus among development actors that capacity is the ability of individuals, institutions and societies to solve problems, make informed choices, define their priorities and plan their futures. Capacity comprises of the resources, knowledge, and processes employed by the organization to achieve its goals. These comprise the staffing, physical infrastructure, technology, and financial resources; strategic leadership, program and process management; and networks and linkages with other organizations and groups. An organization's personnel, facilities, technology, and funding constitute its resource base. The organization's procedures and processes for managing its resources and programs as well as its external relationships make up its management capacity. Together, these resources and management capacities make up the overall capacity of the organization.

2.2 Capacity Building

Capacity Building or capacity development was an issue of development for decades that is tied to international development assistance of the 1950s and 1960s (Farrell, 2007; Simillie, 2001). It was highly oriented to tackle short term technical constraints to project implementation with focus on human resource development, equipping developing countries with a basic inventory of public sector institutions and, later, strengthening them to improve their performance through training, research, counterpart relationships and technical assistance, and political imperative was not given due attention in effecting change (Leautier, et.al., 2010; Smillie, 2001; World Bank, 2005; OECD, 2006).

However, in many poor countries much of the assistance yielded very low returns. Four decades of foreign technical assistance could not result in the achievement of sustainable national capacity and prevented the utilization and development of endogenous skills that resulted in the rethinking of traditional model of knowledge and skills transfer (Leautier, et.al., 2010; Lusthaus, et.al., 1999; Fukuda-Parr, et.al., 2002; OECD, 2006; World Bank, 2005).

As a result, the concept of capacity development emerged in 1980s to gain a high prominence and wide range of popularity throughout 1990s in the field of development building on previous concepts that had dominated development thinking for the past four decades, that includes, institution building, institutional development, human resource development, development management/administration and institutional strengthening by adding new features (such as private sector, and NGOs) into its focus (Lusthaus, et.al., 1999; Koning, et.al., 2006; Smillie, 2001; Lavergne and Saxby, 2001). Capacity building or development was considered as a long term process of restructuring and institutional change with more focus on adaptability and responsiveness of development institutions, and moved beyond the framework of individual organizations, to address about sectoral perspectives and groups of institutions, and began to emphasize on the issue of sustainability (Smillie, 2001).

However the concept continued to be elusive, complex and difficult to understand and operationalize in the design, execution and evaluation of development initiatives. This was due to the fact that the concept was evolved from a wide range of previous approaches (Lavergne and Saxby, 2001). Moreover, the definitional problem of capacity building has to do with the target and purpose. In some cases individuals, a community, or an organizations are to be strengthened. In others, the target is a sector, such as agricultural or health, while in others the target may be an entire societal subset. Capacity building may also be a means to an end while in others the end may be more important than the means. In some cases the process of capacity building may be more important than either the means or the ends. Some describe capacity building as an approach or process to achieve a goal, such as poverty reduction, while others see it as an objective in itself, such as the development of individual or organization effectiveness (Farrell,

2007; Smillie, 2001; Ubels, et.al., 2010). Whatever the purpose and targets of capacity building or capacity development might be here are some among several conceptions and definitions.

Capacity development is a dynamic process whereby different actors (individuals, groups, institutions and organizations) on different levels try to improve their abilities in relation to each other, and identify and meet development challenges overtime (Koning, et.al., 2006; Morgan, 1997; UNDP, 1997; Smillie, 2001; Lavergne and Saxby, 2001). This definition entails that capacity building is a process on its own right. Capacity building is understood as something that individuals, groups, organizations and societies can achieve on themselves. This implies that outsiders can reinforce or support the process but they cannot deliver the final outcomes. In connection with this (OECD, 2006; UNDP, 1997; Horton, 2002) defined capacity development as the process by which individuals, groups, organizations, institutions and societies increase their abilities to (i) perform core functions, solve problems, define and achieve objectives; and (ii) understand and deal with their development needs in a broad context and in a sustainable manner. It is about community's ability to appreciate organizational goals, and to build and use its resources to that end.

Capacity development is about ability of individuals, organizations and societies to set goals and achieve them; to budget resources and use them for agreed purposes; and to manage the complex processes and interactions that typify a working political and economic system. Capacity is most tangibly and effectively developed in the context of specific development objectives such as delivering services to poor people; instituting education, public service, and healthcare reform; improving the investment climate for small and medium enterprises; empowering local communities to better participate in public decision-making processes; and promoting peace and resolving conflict. In addition to government, the capacity of the private sector and civil society to participate meaningfully in the development process, in turn to provide employment and hold government to account is considered as vital. Capacity development is largely an internal process of growth and development, and that capacity development efforts should be result oriented (World Bank, 2005; ACBF, 2011).

Capacity building is a process of unleashing, strengthening, creating, adapting and maintaining capacity overtime (OECD, 2006; World Bank, 2005). It is an ongoing process by which people and systems, operating within dynamic contexts, enhance their abilities to develop and implement strategies in pursuit of their objectives for increased performance in a sustainable way (Lusthaus, et.al., 1999). Capacity development involves the long term, contributes to sustainable social and economic development, and is or should be demand driven. It encompasses a variety of strategies that have to do with increasing and strengthening the efficiency, effectiveness and responsiveness of governments or institutions to design, implement and evaluate development activities according to their mission. Capacity development tends to be a continuing learning and changing process. The concept of capacity development was attached with the needs and purposes of organizations that it is the ability of institutions to identify and solve development problems overtime. It is task driven and mission oriented referring to capacity to perform certain functions. Capacity development is about an effort to change a society's rules, situations and standards of behavior (UNDP, 1997; Malik, 2002).

Capacity development involves the acquisition of new knowledge and its application in the pursuits of individual and organizational goals. Accordingly, it can be targeted at gaps and weaknesses in the following: resources, skills and knowledge, organization, politics and power, incentives (Brinkerhoff, 2010). It is the process by which people of a given society are motivated to transform their physical, socio-economic, cultural, political, and spiritual environments for their own well-being and the advancement of their society. It is about empowering people to take control of their lives and enables people to rediscover their strengths and limitations, and the opportunities to develop their fullest potential. The process enables people to build self-confidence and self-respect, and to improve the quality of their lives, utilizing their own resources, both human and nonhuman. The African Capacity Building Foundation (2011), states that capacity development seeks to enlarge the people's choice by empowering individuals, groups, organizations and societies to fully participate and deliver on their specified mandates. It ensures that there is a room for them to participate in their country's decision making and economy. Capacity building aims at enhancing the ability to evaluate and address the crucial questions related to policy choices and modes of implementation among development options based on an understanding of environment potentials and limits and of needs perceived by the people of the country concerned.

Capacity development entails sustainable creation, utilization and retention of that capacity to reduce poverty, enhance self-reliance, and improve people's lives. It requires acquisition of individual skills, institutional capacities and social capital, and equipping a country, a region, an organization or an individual with attitudes, values, behaviors that they needed to make progress as well as the development of opportunities to put these skills and networks to productive use in the transformation of society (Farrell, 2007; World Bank, 2005; Fowler and Ubels, 2010; Fukuda-Parr, et.al., 2002; Lavergne and Saxby, 2001; Gbla and Rugumamu 2003). It is not only about acquisition of knowledge and enhancing knowledge and skills of individuals but it is also the capability to use them. Capacity is not only about skills and procedures; it is also about incentives and governance (OECD, 2006).

Capacity development is about altering the access of people to authority, resources and opportunities. It privileges some individuals and groups not others. It is a process of unlocking or inducing the potential capacity of country or sector or group or individual that they had within themselves. Capacity development is about transformation from one pattern of behavior to another. In this way it is about the dynamic of organizational, institutional, personal, political, and logistic change (Baser and Morgan, 2008).Capacity development is important in that it helps to trigger economic growth and development. It is a process of creating opportunities for people to be creative and imaginative, to dream, and to be able to live their dreams (Turay, 2001).

Capacity building involves the whole network of relationships in society: within, between and among households, neighborhoods, grassroots or community-based organizations, unions, religious confessions, training institutions, research bodies, government ministries, the private sector, NGOs and donor agencies—whether official or nongovernmental, Northern or Southern (Eade , 2003).

It seems, therefore, that there is an emerging consensus that capacity development is a long term process that contributes to sustainable economic and social development. It also entails that capacity development is about strengthening and enhancement of existing capacity as opposed to the past approach of institutional building which emphasis on establishing new institutions based on the experience from industrialized countries of the west. Capacity development is also a response to the structural and functional disconnect between informal, endogenous institutions and formal institutions mostly transplanted from outside. Capacity development aims to increase the ability of an organization to carry out its functions and achieve its objectives. It increases the ability of an organization to learn and solve problems as well as to deal with the issues of today and also to remain relevant in the future (Lusthaus, et.al., 1999; Lavergne and Saxby, 2001).

2.2.1 Dimensions of Capacity Building or Capacity Development

Capacity building or capacity development which involves the interaction between or among different actors (individuals, organizations, institutions, and society) comprises of different dimensions or aspects which are mutually interdependent.

2.2.1.1 Individual Development

Individual development involves enabling individuals to engage in continuous process of learning which is building on existing knowledge and skills, and extending these in new directions as fresh opportunities appear (Fukuda-Parr, et.al., 2002; Gbla and Rugumamu, 2003). The dimensions at individual level will include the design of educational and training programs and courses to meet the identified gaps within the skills base, experience and knowledge vested in the people, training of trainers and the number of qualified staff to operate the systems (Koning, et.al., 2006; ACBF, 2011). It addresses the need for individuals to function efficiently and effectively within the entity and within the broader system.

Capacity-building involves establishing the conditions under which public servants are able to embark on a continuous process of learning and adapting to change — building on existing knowledge and skills and enhancing and using them in new directions. This requires a new approach to human resources management and also points to the importance of knowledge management as the new vehicle for increased learning (UN, 2006). Education, on job training, and formal and informal skills development to accomplish tasks and solve problems are core requirements. It is about participating individuals in decision making and having a clear understanding of their role and function. It is about individuals' incentives, salary structures and accountability. Values, expectations and power relations need to be considered. The emphasis is on continuous and incremental learning, formal and informal training, skills development, improved human resource policies, incentives and improved information and accountability systems (UNDP, 1997).

2.2.1.2 Organizational Development

Focuses on organizational structures, processes, resources, and management styles that affect how individual talents and skills are used to accomplish particular tasks. It should be pointed out that organizations establish goals, structure work, define authority relations and provide incentives and disincentives that shape behavior of those who work within them (Gbla and Rugumamu, 2003). The dimensions of capacity at organizational level includes areas like mission and strategy, culture and competencies, human resources planning and management, technical and management processes, reorientations of government agencies, processes of decentralization, internal policies, procedures and frameworks that allows organizations to operate and deliver on their mandate and that enable the integration of to work together and achieve goals, external relations, resources and infrastructure (Koning, et.al., 2006; ACBF, 2011). At this level all dimensions of capacity should be examined including its interaction within the system, with other entities, stakeholders and clients.

It is the elaboration of management structures, processes and procedures, not only within organizations but also the management of relationships between the different organizations and sectors (public, private and community) (CHIP, 2007). Organizational capacity involves groups of individuals bound by a common purpose, with clear objectives and the internal structures, processes, systems, staffing, and other resources to achieve them (World Bank, 2005). It entails that working within or with an entity that has clear organizational structure, mission, goals, functions, systems and resources requires a well-trained, productive person that needs access to finance, technology, information, infrastructure and other resources. Hence, the key capacity requirements to be assessed at the organizational level include: vision and mission, strategy, policies and values, competencies and functions, processes (internal and external), human resources and financial information and physical resources (UNDP, 1997).

2.2.1.3 Institutional Development

Institution entails rules, laws, norms, regulations, and incentives by which the behavior of individuals and organizations can be influenced (Koning, et.al., 2006). Similar to the individual levels, rather than establishing or creating new institutions on foreign blue prints it is better to seek out existing initiatives, and encourage the existing institutions to grow (Fukuda-Parr et.al.,

2002; Gbla and Rugumamu, 2003; UN, 2006). This dimension includes current policies, public service laws, bye-laws, rules and regulations, budgetary allocations, the role of the state and its financial resources, and formal and informal power relationships such as practices of corruption, making legal and regulatory changes to enable organizations, institutions and agencies at all levels and in all sectors to enhance their capacities (Peltenburg, et. al., 1996; CHIP, 2007; Brinkerhoff, 2010).

Institutional capacity comprises of the formal 'rules of the game' and informal norms—for example, in collecting taxes, reporting on the use of public resources, or regulating private business—that provide the framework of goals and incentives within which organizations and people operate (World Bank, 2005; UN, 2006). Development policies and plans, legal frameworks, ability and willingness reform, distribution of institutional responsibilities, public sector and human resource policies, incentives and so on. These requirements include policies; strategies; legislation; and capabilities to coordinate, manage changes and implement programs (UNDP, 1997).

2.2.1.4 Human Resource Development

Human resource development is the process of equipping individuals with the understanding, skills and access to information, design and implement strategies, policies and programs; deliver services, and monitor results knowledge and training that enables them to perform effectively and analyze development needs (CHIP, 2007; World Bank, 2005). It is related to training and recruitment of managerial, professional, and technical talent that contributes to organizational performance (Gbla and Rugumamu, 2003). Local capacity building is about empowering people to make a difference in their own communities (Smillie, 2001).

According to Mackay, et.al. (2002), developing human capacities must include the emotional, intellectual, psychological, cultural, spiritual, and social needs of people. Capacity building must therefore be based on the lived experiences, aspirations, resources, needs, visions, and limitations of the local people. It is about assisting the marginalized and oppressed in society to take ownership and control of their development process. Human resource capacity is essential to improve and make optimal use of the total knowledge, creative abilities, skills, talents and attitudes of an organization's working force.

Human resource management involves the planning, implementation and monitoring of the organization's labor force. Human resource management involves the forecasting of the human resource needs of the organization, and planning the steps necessary to meet these needs (human resource planning); identifying the kinds of human resources that it needs to perform well (staffing human resources); improving employee performance by increasing or improving their skills, knowledge and attitudes through on job-training, education, and others (human resource development); and distribution of rewards (direct and indirect, monetary and non-monetary) within the legal regulations of the organizations (rewarding human resources).

It has been recognized that in addition to the training the functioning of individuals are dependent on a number of other factors. One of the most important is motivation. Others include as pay-scales, conditions of employment, career perspectives and office facilities and working conditions. Education and training are the most important but not the only means of human resource development (Peltenburg, et.al., 1996).

Moreover, an organization's performance depends not only upon its financial, human, and other resources but also on its managers' capacity to plan, set goal, determine responsibilities and lead, motivate and supervise staff members, and maintaining relations with stakeholders allocate and deploy these resources in the successful pursuit of its strategic goals.

2.2.1.5 Societal Development

It encompasses transforming the whole society. It involves widening the opportunities of people to expand and use their knowledge to the fullest whether in the public or private sector. Social capital and cohesions are at the heart of societal capacity. With this regard, Woodhill (2010), argue that capacity is not just a matter of individual skills or internal organizational arrangements. These factors might be relevant building blocks – some would call these competencies or capabilities – but they do not constitute real capacity. Effective capacity is visible and exists when people identify and act on issues of shared concern. Hence, with the absence of such opportunities the skills of the people will deteriorate and become obsolete which results in trained and skilled people join the brain drain and take their skills overseas (Gbla and Rugumamu, 2003; Fukuda-Parr. et.al., 2002; Browne, 2002).

Capacity development at the societal level is required to support the paradigm of a more interactive public administration that learns equally from its actions and from the feedback it receives from the population at large (UN, 2006). It encompasses the facilitatory processes which lie at the heart of human development: the opening and widening of opportunities that enable people to use and expand their capacities to the fullest (Browne, 2002).

Capacity at this level includes a number of areas such as an appropriate national policy framework, planning, improved legislation and regulations, a changed perspective on management and accountability, (other) conceptual innovations and the resources available (Koning, et.al., 2006).

2.2.2 Factors that Determines the Success of Capacity Building or Capacity Development

Capacity building aims at improving and enhancing the capacity of individuals, organizations, institutions, and society in realms of setting goals and objectives, and attaining them through responding to the challenges and constraints on their way to realize their goals. The realization of this aim requires different conditions and settings that facilitate or constraints capacity building efforts.

2.2.2.1 Internally Initiated and Demand Driven

The failure of the previous attempt at building capacity was mostly attributed to lack of country ownership. With this regard, the World Bank Task Force on Capacity Development in Africa (2005) argues that African states and their international partners have long focused on supply-side measures: improvements in public sector skills and management, supported by technical assistance in the form of training and blueprint organizational and procedural change. However, the 2005 Paris Declaration recognized capacity development as a necessarily endogenous process, strongly led from within a country, with donors playing a supporting role. Capacity building efforts will succeed only where they take adequate account of the prevailing local politics and institutions, and are country owned rather than donor. An effective state develops capacity from within, driven by supply, and in response to external pressures, driven by demand (OECD, 2006; Walters, 2003; World Bank, 2005).

2.2.2.2 Strong Political leadership and Commitment

Political leadership is the primary driver of capacity development. Where major policies and institutions are involved, strong political commitment is required to introduce change. Capacity development is a long process that hinges on strong and legitimate leadership with clear vision and strategies, willing to take risks, and depend on existing capacities, assets, and systems (World Bank, 2005). Accordingly, vision, political leadership and the prevailing political and governance system are critical factors in creating opportunities and setting limits for capacity development effort. Moreover, policies are determined in large part by the qualities and commitments of leaders. Leadership is important as development is a process of transformation, and capacities continually need to change and adapt. Strong leadership – and the strategic vision that goes with it are necessary to anticipate change and adjust to it (Browne, 2002).

2.2.2.3 The Prevailing System of Governance and Policy Environment

Approaches to capacity have to take in to account the link between governance and the policy environment on the one hand and capacity development and its effective use on the other. In the words of the World Bank Task Force on Capacity Development in Africa (2005), the capacity challenge is fundamentally a governance challenge. Governance is considered as crucial matters for capacity development. UNDP's experience also shows that capacity development is most sustainable when programs are: responsive to the needs of people and stakeholders; participatory throughout the process; built on the free flow of information (transparent); equitable; accountable (decision makers in government, the private sector and civil society are accountable to the public as well as to institutional stakeholders); consensus – oriented (differing interests are mediated on what is in the best interest of the whole group); effective and efficient (individuals, processes and institutions produce results that meet those needs, while making the best use of resources); strategic (based on long-term societal vision and reflecting analysis of full range of opportunities and strengths) (UNDP, 1997). Thus, political and economic governance- including the rule of law and accountability and transparency of the executive, the legislature, and the judiciary provides substantial support for capacity development and retention.

Policy environment highly influence capacity development. Policies can facilitate and restrain the ability of individuals and organizations to perform. The policy environment is critical to capacity development. But the mere enunciation of good policy is not enough. It must be consistently and transparently enacted, for which there need to be capacities for implementation, and mechanisms of objective inspection, monitoring and audit systems (Browne, 2002).

2.2.2.4 The Broader Environment

The processes of capacity building are embedded in complex environments that either constraint or help achieve the intended objective. The broader environments of capacity building constitute the political economy environment. It includes the political, economic, and social milieu (local, national and international) in which individuals, groups, organizations and societies undertake their set of objectives that either facilitate or constraint their performance (Gbla and Rugumamu, 2003; UNDP, 1997; Brinkerhoff, 2010). Some of these are competencies or capabilities themselves which can be the object of capacity building initiatives, while others are contextual variables that capacity building interventions may or may not be able to influence (Farrell, 2007).

Successful capacity development is associated with two sets of factors. First, there is a set of broad enabling conditions that increase the likelihood of success. These may include an external environment that is conducive to change; top managers who provide leadership for institutional change; a critical mass of staff members involved in, and committed to, the change process; sound policies, high levels of commitment, effective coordination, and a stable economic environment; favorable incentives, availability or development of appropriate institutional innovations; adequate resources for developing capacities and implementing changes; adequate management of the capacity development process, peace and economic growth, and trends in politics and society resulting in the institutionalization of improved governance and an increase in the legitimacy and influence of formal rules as against informal patronage (Horton, 2002; Farrell, 2007; OECD, 2006; Turay, 2001; Smillie, 2001; UNDP, 1997). According to Olowu and Wunsch (2004), legal reform to support the establishment of local governance is only the first step. For the intentions expressed in law to become certain requires a supportive national political context, an effective system of intergovernmental relations, and strong local demand for public goods along with substantial levels of local social capital and well-designed local institutions.

Second, Poorly conceived policies, high levels of corruption, or lack of legitimacy, lack of human security and presence of armed conflict, poor economic policy that discourages pro-poor growth; weak parliamentary scrutiny of the executive branch; lack of effective voice or participation, and unclear and arbitrarily enforced laws, rules and policies; poor overall capacity for economic and public financial management, and low levels of transparency and accountability; rapidly changing government policies, and overload of reform and change initiatives; unpredictable, unbalanced or inflexible funding and staffing; poor public service conditions: salary levels incompatible with reasonable expectations of living standards; flight of qualified staff to other countries; excessive reliance on donor-funded positions, lack of rewards for performance and of sanctions for non-performance are factors that deteriorates capacity building efforts (OECD, 2006; Farrell, 2007; World Bank, 2005; UNDP, 1997).

2.2.2.5 Availability and Management of Resources

A society's capacity to meet the needs of its members depends on the resources available to it, and largely on to how best those resources are utilized. Developing capacity with inadequate financial resources and physical infrastructure results in trained people and organizations without the budget and facilities to do their job. Available and coordinated resources for managing change, developing capacities, capital investment and recurrent costs are critical (UNDP, 1997). The resources available to the society are wide ranging and more or less tangible in nature. Accordingly, there are two types of resources that serve as an input to capacity development or capacity building.

Tangible resources are mostly found at the bottom of organizational hierarchy, they are measurable, quantifiable, and visible and they can easily be grasped and worked with that comprises of material and financial resources, skills, organizational structures and systems, physical assets such as infrastructure, plant and machinery and natural resources. These may also include resources that can be described in structural terms or as tangible forms of information and analysis. Examples of this are organizational structures and systems, legal frameworks and policies, books, reports and the like (Lavergne and Saxby, 2001; Kaplan, 2000).

Besides, there are wide ranges of less tangible but not less important dimensions of capacity that belongs to the top of organizational hierarchy and is invisible. They are observable only through the effects they have to the organizations and to the practitioners. They are ephemeral, transitory, not easily assessed or weighed. They constitutes skills, experience and creativity; social cohesion and social capital; values and motivations; habits and traditions; institutional culture and etc. These intangible dimensions of capacity are crucial as they determine how well the society uses the other resources at its disposal (Lavergne and Saxby, 2001; Kaplan, 2000).Hence, capacity development needs to embed both types of resources as they are equally important in developing capacity.

Therefore, building effective local governance places a high emphasis on the prevailing environment, local ownership with political leadership and the prevailing political and governance system, in creating opportunities and setting limits for capacity development efforts, and requires local autonomy and authority, sufficient resources, participatory, and an open and accountable local political process.

2.3 Capacity Building for Decentralized Local Governments

Recently decentralization and local governance have become vital concerns by several national governments of developing countries. This also reflects the fact that effective local government is critical to improving access to social and infrastructure services and to mobilize local resources. However, the pervasive weakness of local governments and their institutions, and their lack of capacity are recognized by many as major impediment to social and economic development. Even though local governments have great potential to attain economic development objectives, they lack capacity to perform as expected in developing countries (Yigremew, et.al., 2005). Technical, managerial, financial and organizational skills are all needed to ensure adequate performance and sustainability of local governments over longer term.

Based on a study of local governments in Colombia, the World Bank (1996) has outlined three conditions that make possible for local governments to perform in an effective way. The quality of its staff which depends on both their skills and the way they are utilized within the bureaucratic structure (labor); the equipment, material and buildings required in public sector activities, without which quality labor could become ineffective (capital); and the governments' internal organization and management style, planning and execution of functions. Accordingly, local governments with capacity need to have the necessary and major resources to function and carry out their assigned authority and responsibilities. Skilled human resources, infrastructures and overall organizational structure and management style are considered as a key ingredient to the effective performance of local governments.

Moreover, the United Nations Center for Regional Development (UNCRD, 1996) on the basis of its study of local governments in Asia and Latin America, identified six indicators for effective local government: a legal mandate that matches local organizational and resource capacity; institutional structures that enhance local autonomy (in terms of organizational capacity and decision making); a flexible managerial approach which induce local governments to faithfully carry out policy or program initiatives (defining clear areas of responsibility between central and local agencies; for example, the acquisition of managerial, planning, and technical skills, knowledge and experience for program planning and implementations; the ability to finance local economic development initiatives by generating revenues locally and tapping external resources; and the ability to manage the local economy and initiate development activities within the framework of national policy goals.

Hence, capacity building or capacity development is the most critical factor for effective local governance. Capacity development requires local governments to undertake reforms in the way they conduct their operations, to make investment in human resources and equipment, to adopt new work practices; and for this efforts to occur, innovation and responsible leadership and community participation provides the required motivation and the principal elements. Local capacity development needs, therefore, have to give attention to areas such as staff skills and professionalization, equipment, materials and buildings, access to adequate financial resources, organization and the administration's planning and execution, local autonomy, creation of flexible managerial approaches and legal reforms so that the performance of local governance can improve.

2.4 Decentralization and Capacity Building in Ethiopia

Ethiopia's experience in decentralization and local governance is very limited. The country has been under a highly centralized system with very little powers and responsibilities for local governments. Local governments in Ethiopia were not autonomous organs with full control over resources and with adequate decision-making; rather they acted as field agents of central governments for a long time.

Except for the deconcentrated and delegated forms of decentralization observed during the previous two regimes, Ethiopia has been a unitary state with strict centralization of authority and responsibility until 1991. In spite of the existence of woredas and *awrajas* as sub national tiers of government structure, their roles in providing public services were limited as the central government was responsible for providing services at the local level and the local governments were powerless and could not participate in local development (Mehret, 2002; Vander Loop, 2002; Yigremew, 2001). Under both the Imperial and Derg regime, thus, very little effort was made to decentralize power.

The governmental change that took place in 1991, however, changed the political and socio-economic landscape in the country. As a result, the country adopted federal system of governance through promulgation of the 1995 constitution that created nine national regional states and two administrative cities on the basis of ethnically delineated border that laid the foundation for decentralization as they are responsible for broad ranges of the country's political, economic and social objectives (Vander Loop, 2002; Meheret, 2002; Tegegne and Kassahun, 2004; Tegegne, 2007). However, woredas roles and responsibilities were not clearly defined; they enjoyed little fiscal autonomy to respond to local needs, and were deconcentrated units of regions until 2001. Systematic constraints in human and institutional capacity, poor economic management and governance, inadequate accountability and transparency of woredas remains amongst core problems that act as impediment to sustainable growth and poverty reduction (Fenta, 1998; Mehret, 2002; Yigremew et.al., 2005; Vander Loop, 2002).

In order to further deepen the already initiated decentralization and overcome the above mentioned short comings of decentralization the second phase of decentralization was launched through devolution of power in financial and human resources to woredas (Dickovick and Tegegne, 2010; Tegegne, 2007; Zemelak, 2009). To facilitate the decentralization program and improve the delivery of services at local level, various reform programs have also been introduced. A comprehensive National Capacity Building Program (NCBP) was launched to respond to the capacity building demands of the country. Ministry of Capacity Building was established in 2001 to ensure good governance, transparency and accountability and to create the conditions for a more active role of the public, private and civil society.

Public Sector Capacity Building Program (PSCAP) has also been launched in 2004 as part of the concerted effort to the on-going capacity building initiatives with the objective of building national capacity across regions and sectors over the medium-term as an integral part of Sustainable Development and Poverty Reduction Programs (SDPRP). Capacity building under PSCAP includes support for the development of human resource through delivery of huge on job training across public organizations, development of working systems, and improvement in the effectiveness of institutions. The National Capacity Building Program (NCBP) targets 14 sectors: civil service reform, tax reform, justice reform, district decentralization, information and communication technology, private sector, construction sector, urban management, cooperatives, textile and garments, agricultural training of vocational and technical levels, industrial training of vocational and technical levels, civil society, and higher education (Dickovick and Tegegne, 2010; Yigremew, et.al., 2005). Out of the fourteen sub-programs six of them are concerned with strengthening and building capacity in core parts of the public sector and have been grouped under PSCAP (Yigremew, et.al., 2005; Worku, 2005). They include civil service reform, district level decentralization program (DLDP), justice system reform, information communication, tax reform, and urban management.

Local government capacity building in rural areas is addressed by the District Level Decentralization Program. Capacity Building under DLDP was launched to bring about changes and improvements in Woreda institutional structure, working systems for planning and implementation and service delivery, and manpower development. Thus, the overall objectives of DLDP is to enhance the institutions, working systems and human capital in an integrated and coordinated manner at woreda and *kebele* levels to ensure democratization, empowerment and good governance.

The specific objectives of DLDP includes fulfilling the required manpower for the public institution; and training in areas critical to local government to enhance the capacity of public servants, electorates and other stakeholders at woreda and Kebele levels including human resource policies, procedures, and plans; and to establish efficient and effective structure at woreda and kebele level through institutional and organization development including assessment of functional assignments and enabling legislation, assistance in establishing structures and restructuring existing arrangements including local level accountability relationships.

Moreover, DLDP aims at establishing the system of broad based participation and empowerment of the grassroots population through technical assistance and training for grassroots participation including the development of guidelines and monitoring mechanisms, and the strengthening of civil society involvement at the local level. Furthermore, capacity building for policy and program development including technical assistance for woreda decentralization strategy and policy development, benchmarking and review of plans; establishing systems for clear accountability, transparency, and relationships of executives were emphasized.

Besides, establishing minimum service indicators or standards for basic sectors and monitor the systems to facilitate the delivery of services at Woreda and Kebele levels; development of woreda fiscal transfer mechanisms and revenue mobilization capacities through the review and design of various intergovernmental fiscal instruments; and enhancing capacity for planning and execution with the introduction of improved woreda planning manual; and ensuring the effectiveness of budget preparation and control system through strengthening of the planning system & financial management at the woreda level were the main objectives of DLDP (Yigremew, etal., 2005; MoFED, 2002; UNDP/UNCDF, 2005; FDRE, 2007).

The implementation of DLDP is divided into two phases of three and four years each. First phase (2002-2004) comprises initial intervention in selected woredas of all regions. Second phase (2005-2008) involves deepening and consolidation of capacity building activities in the four advanced regions and continuing initial interventions as well as deepening and consolidation in the remaining four regions. Therefore, the activities of DLDP planned for the five-year period were categorized under enabling, deepening, and consolidation stages (UNDP/UNCDF, 2005; Yigremew, 2005).

As a result, powers and responsibilities have been devolved to woredas since 2001. The revised regional constitution of Oromia National Regional State also defined the duties and responsibilities of the woredas in the region. The responsibility for planning, budgeting, and implementation of public service delivery were given to woredas. Woreda administrations have been given autonomy in expenditure prioritization when planning basic services. According to the revised constitution of Oromia National Regional State, chapter nine Article 76-89, woredas are empowered to deliver basic services such as agricultural extension, education, health, water supply and rural roads. Woreda empowerment was enhanced by transfer of functions, finance and human resources from regional and zonal levels. A regional block grant was introduced in the fiscal year 2002/2003 and intended to finance woreda salaries, operational and capital development projects. Woredas were also restructured and reorganized and a large number of staff has also been made in view of the weak performing capacities observed in the processes of woreda decentralization (Worku, 2005).

Therefore, in order to deepen decentralization to local level and to create a well-functioning decentralized local governance and civil service, building local capacity is one of the most important factors. Strengthening the already existing local institutions and their human resources' technical and management capacity, as well as creating new ones are of paramount importance. The capacity of local government and local institutions is a function of a complex mixes of skills, knowledge and experiences as well as capacity of both human and financial capital. The presence of proper institutional capacity and administrative authority devolved for decision making processes at local level is of critical advantage to strengthen the local governments' capacity in executing responsibilities and achieve its development goal.

Chapter Three

Data Presentation and Analysis

3.1. Description of the Study Areas

3.1.1. Gindeberet Woreda Profile

Gindeberet Woreda is located in south western part of Oromia National Regional State. The Woreda is situated at an altitude of 2600m above sea level and at a distance of 180KM from Addis Ababa. It is bordered by Yejube Woreda in North, Jeldu, Elfeta, and Ambo in South, Abuna Gindeberet in East and Midakegne and Ababoguduru Woreda in the West. Administratively, the woreda is divided into 32 Kebele Administrations, 31 rural and 1 urban, out of which 17 Kebeles are found in Kola, where most of them are food in secured. Ten (10) Kebeles in middle highland and 5 in lowland are considered as potential (surplus producers).

According to the recent (2007) census result, the total population of the Woreda is 107,844, of which male and female account to 48.5% and 51.5% respectively. About 87% of the total population resides in the rural area, whereas the remaining 13% are urban dwellers. The numbers of households are estimated to be 17, 736, while 15% of them are estimated to be female headed. Protestant and Orthodox are the dominant religion in the area. Ethnically, it consists of Oromo and Amhara ethnic groups, the former making the majority. The livelihood of the community is mainly based on mixed farming, crop and livestock husbandry.

Its topography is mainly made up of conspicuous rugged to undulating landscape in the lowland and with flat plateau in the mid highland. The area is categorized into two agro climatic zones, where mid highland and lowland accounts to 43% and 57% respectively. The average annual rainfall ranges from 800mm in the lowland to 1600mm in the highland, with an average temperature of 18.5^0c. The land use system of the Woreda under the study indicates that 50.3% cultivated land, 40.2% grazing, 2.5% bush and forest, and 7% others.

The population of the Woreda generally lacks access to basic social services. According to the secondary data, although the access of the community to education facilities have been sustainably improved, the quality of learning and teaching is worst. Most of the classes are built up of wood and with no appropriate desks. The access to the potable water is also highly limited.

According to the Woreda report, the safe water coverage is only 27%. There are three health stations, one rural hospital, and 62 health extension workers each kebele having two workers.

With respect to social facilities, there are two banks (Oromia International Bank and Commercial Bank of Ethiopia), 24 hours hydroelectric power supplies, and town water supplies that do not provide services and other social facilities are available in the capital town of the Woreda (Kachisi).

3.1.2. Abuna Gindeberet Woreda Profile

Abuna Gindeberet Woreda was previously been one of Gindeberet woreda's Kebele administrations. However, in 1998 E.C. by taking the number of its population and the area of the woreda and the demand of the community into account the Oromia National Regional State has decided the previous Kebele to be Woreda administration. It was bordered by Meta Robi Woreda in East, Gindeberet Woreda in West, Jeldu Woreda in South, and Amhara National Regional State in North. It is situated at an altitude of 1000m-2064m above sea level with a distance of 184KM from the capital city of the country, Addis Ababa. Abuna Gindeberet Woreda is divided into 44 Kebele Administrations out of which 42 of them are rural Kebeles while 2 of them are town administrations.

If one looks at its demographic composition, the recent (2007) census result demonstrates that the Woreda comprises the total population of 126,996 out of which 47.2% are male while the remaining 52.8% population are female. 98% of the population is using agriculture as a means of livelihood while 2% of them are public servants and small traders. The Woreda has 19,713 male and 2,913 female householders.

The Woreda is categorized into 2 agro climatic zones, where mid highland and lowland accounts to 32 and 68% consecutively. The Woreda receives an average annual rainfall that ranges from 700mm in the lowland to 2400mm in the highland, with an average temperature that ranges from $10^{0}c$ minimum to $30^{0}c$ maximum. The land use system of the Woreda shows that 87,784.25 hectare is cultivable land, about 36,726 hectare forest and bush, while 12,026 hectare land constitute grazing land and finally, about 1,947 hectare covers the remaining area. The safe water coverage constitutes 36%.

The population of the Woreda generally has limited access to social services. The Woreda under study, has 7 animal and 6 human heath stations. In terms of education service, the Woreda has 36, grade 5-8, 12, grade 1-4 and 1 secondary schools respectively.

3.2. Data Analysis and Interpretation

3.2.1. Power and Structures of Woredas

The 2001 Oromia National Regional State Constitution that was enacted to revise the functions and responsibilities of woredas clearly puts in chapter nine (Article 76-89) the organization, and duties and functions of woredas as follows. Woredas comprises of three main organs that include, District Council-which is the highest government organ of the district organized below 'Caffee' that embraces the representative of the people in each kebele which are accountable to their electorate; District Administrative Council-is the executive organ of the district that encompasses of the district administrator, deputy administrator, and the head of the main sectoral executive offices found in the district which are ultimately accountable to the district administrator and district council; and District Judicial organ.

Moreover, the constitution stipulates different duties and functions that woredas should undertake. Among other things woredas are vested to prepare, approve, and implement and control plans and programs with regard to economic development, social service and public administration of the district; protect, preserve, develop and oversee natural resource development and mobilization as well as basic agricultural development; ensure the proper collection of land use taxes, agricultural products' income taxes and other taxes; create conducive condition to mobilize and activate the public for development activities; issue and implement directives to ensure the maintenance of peace and security in the district and direct the district police and security forces; implement the policies, laws, directives, plans and programs of the state in the district; prepare, approve and implement its budget plan; and utilize revenues other than those that fall within the domain of the regional state (Oromia National Regional State Megeleta Oromia, 2008).

Hence, the woreda enjoys substantial authority to decide on social and economic development plans as well as generation and utilization of own of revenues. The woreda is responsible for supervision, coordination and implementation of education services, health services, agricultural services, rural roads, water supply and sanitation, rural transport services, justice, information etc. within its jurisdiction.

However, practically woredas have been restricted in terms of fully exercising its devolved powers particularly in personnel administration. With this regard, woredas autonomy to hire and dismiss employee is revoked beginning from this fiscal year (2011/2012) as zonal administration are empowered to hire and fire Bachelor degree level and above while woredas are entitled to hire supporting staffs with the prior approval of the Bureau of Civil Service and Good Governance while diploma level remained to be under the jurisdictions of any tiers of government. This has created a mismatch between the human resource needs of woredas and the assigned employee/positions. An interview with Bureau of Civil Service and Good Governance indicates that the mandate was withdrawn due to the complexity of the work and the inability of woredas. The other issue worth mentioning is that the proportion of recurrent budget to capital budget is decided by the regional government.

Moreover, strategies to achieve the goals and objectives of every sectoral offices also emanates from the regional government that resulted in lack of awareness and resistances to the strategy on the part of employee. Furthermore, the strategies do not stay stable, and is subject to frequent revisions and changes, as well as there is the problem of implementing the strategy.

Besides, woredas do not have the autonomy to decide on their budget as the proportion of capital to recurrent budget is decided by the regional government. Furthermore, woredas do not set their local priorities and targets to be addressed rather they are forced to establish it in line with the priorities and targets of the regional and national government.

3.2.2. Human Resource Capacity

There is a fairly widespread agreement that human resource capacity at all government levels is an essential component of decentralization. The success of decentralization demands the development of competent, skilled, experienced and well trained human resources which are critical to carry out the new decentralized responsibilities and functions effectively. It is mostly agreed issue that decentralization in most countries failed due to the presence of poor implementation capacity (Rondinelli, et.al., 1983; Rondinelli, et.al, 1989). In Ethiopia, substantial deficiency of competent and skilled human resources has been identified as factor hindering the promotion of decentralization process (Fenta, 1998: Mehret, 2002; Tegegne and Kassahun, 2004; Dickovick and Tegegne, 2010). To this end, the government identified staffing and training as one of the nine major components of District Level Decentralization Program. Despite this effort many local government offices, departments, and other local level administration are suffering from acute shortage of qualified human resources.

As indicated in Table 1 below Gindeberet and Abuna Gindeberet Woredas are not the exception to this fact. For instance, Gindeberet and Abuna Gindeberet woredas on average have about 45. 7 and 49% office positions are vacant respectively. This illustrates the severity of the problem in both woredas despite the effort of the government to overcome the problem. As a result, this would pose a serious difficulty to successfully accomplish the decentralized responsibilities and functions.

For example, there are several sector offices which have lack of human resources this includes disaster and prevention, culture and tourism, youth and sport in Gindeberet woreda; and woreda road authority, youth and sport, social security in Abuna Gindeberet are just few of woreda sector offices that have severe shortages of human resources with 75%, 70%, 65% and 75%, 76.5%, and 70.6% respectively. Lack of budget, higher attention to hire supporting staffs than professional staffs, continuing expansion of sectors, and unstable work structure (the merging and abolition of sectoral offices) were responsible factors for the presence of vacant positions. Moreover, the five main poverty alleviation sectors that include education, water, road, health, and agriculture also have inadequate human resources. In light of this, in Gindeberet woreda education, water, roads, health and agriculture offices accounted for 35, 57.5, 57, 38.5 and 40 percent are understaffed respectively while in Abuna Gindeberet woreda except the health office which is relatively filled 43.5, 59.5, 75, and 44.2 percent of education, water, road, and agriculture constitute unfilled positions respectively. It is therefore, possible to deduce that both woredas have critical shortage of qualified human resources to carry out their decentralized functions and responsibilities properly.

Moreover, an official document (First Quarter Report on human resources of the Woreda, 2004) exhibits the fact that only 6 Master degree holders are available in Gindeberet Woreda while none at Abuna Gindeberet woreda. Furthermore, 151 and 71 Bachelor Degree holders are available in Gindeberet and Abuna Gindeberet woreda whereas 278 and 169 of the former and later woreda are Diploma holders respectively. Besides, those who have certificates (10+1 and 10+2) level constitute 10 in Abuna Gindeberet woreda and 28 in Gindeberet woreda. The remaining 49 and 64 staffs in Gindeberet and Abuna Gindeberet woredas are composed of grade 10 and 12 complete. Last but not least, Gindeberet and Abuna Gindeberet woredas staffs constitute 30 and 6 below grade 10 respectively. In addition Gindeberet woreda has 28 temporary employees that works for a limited period of time (contract workers). This indicates that more than half of the total employees of the woreda comprises of diploma holders and below as about 51 percent of Gindeberet woreda and 53% of Abuna Gindeberet woreda are composed of diploma holders. From this, one can deduce that local governments under study lacks skilled and competent labor force that able to achieve the woreda mandates successfully. However, it is important to note that Gindeberet woreda is better than Abuna Gindeberet woreda both in terms of quality and quantity of staff.

Human resource development or training is the other dimension of enhancing local governments' capacity through competent, skilled and qualified man powers. This allows local government staffs to be more flexible and adaptable, and increases staff commitment to the organization by enabling them acquires the requisite knowledge and skills that will upgrade their job performance. This therefore, enables improve and make optimal use of the total knowledge, creative abilities, skills, talents and attitudes of existing work forces.

In this regard, training programs were conducted at different time on different issues since District Level Decentralization Program came in to effect in order to enhance the implementing capacity of employees of different levels. Accordingly, the focus group discussion reveals that training programs were held very rarely, are mostly short term, emphasizes on top officials and is mostly supply driven. Even those training programs that were demand driven are not carried out based on the identified training needs. The emphasis on top officials is with the assumption that local government leaders would in turn train the rest of employees however; top level officials are not in a position to do so since they are not willing and lack the necessary skills. As training is mostly provided by higher tiers of governments the criteria for selection of participants are not transparent. However, despite the above mentioned short comings, the training programs are still relevant to improve the performance of staffs in both Gindeberet and Abuna Gindeberet woredas.

In addition to trainings, the functioning of individuals highly rely on a number of other factors like motivation, pay-scales, conditions of employment, career perspectives and office facilities and working conditions. However, it was found that the fragility or weakness of both monetary and non-monetary reward to enhance the moral, and motivate employees for good performance. Due to lack of employee performance evaluation system, there were no promotions and other incentives for good performance that highly deteriorated the commitment, creativity and innovativeness of employee. In the same token, both local governments explained the limited experience of educational opportunity to encourage staff to continue to learn and develop. For instance, only single master degree and about five bachelor degrees were allowed to compete from each woreda at zonal level. Out of which only one or two individuals who won the competition are to be selected that in turn decreased the likelihood of being selected as they compete with individuals from towns, and as there was no affirmative action that is to be considered for remote woredas that created high turnover of employees mainly from health and agriculture sectors. Moreover, employees of both woredas are not happy with the salary scale they are being paid. Furthermore, people are not assigned as per their professions and there are no proper job descriptions which decreased the likely result of being effective to the position they are assigned to. The cumulative effect of these situations discouraged employees and reduced their commitment to the position they held deteriorating the implementing capacity of local governments.

3.2.3. Management Capacity

An organization's performance depends not only upon its financial, and other resources but also on its managers' capacity to plan, set goal, determine responsibilities and lead, motivate and supervise staff members, and maintain relations with stakeholders allocate and deploy these resources in the successful pursuit of its strategic goals. The effective execution of these activities demands developing the skills and abilities of managers. Therefore, before implementing decentralization policies, governments needs to examine the skills and competence of their managers because decentralizing significant amount of power and authorities results into wastage of decentralized resources due to lack of managerial, technical and administrative capacity that requires major commitment on the side of the government to improve and enhance their competence.

To this end, in order to overcome the managerial capacity the Government of Ethiopia has involved into two major activities. First, it has designed to deploy qualified and professional employee from region and zone to local governments. The other strategy to develop managerial capacity was to provide short, medium and long term training activities. However, the survey result in Gindeberet and Abuna Gindeberet woreda showed that the effort of the government seemed to be remained scant. The Table 2 below indicates this fact.

Employees were requested to rate the performance of their employees based on different parameters. For example, they were asked to rate the effort of their managers to build shared vision and mutual goals among employees, and 54 (50%) of Gindeberet woreda and 31 (49.2%) of Abuna Gindeberet woreda employee demonstrated the effort of their managers to set common goals and shared vision as negligible while the remaining 43 (39.8%) and 30 (47.6%) of Gindeberet and Abuna Gindeberet woreda rated the same issue as satisfactory respectively. This lack of mutual vision and goals impede clarity of purpose, a foundation for making decisions and commitment for goals that negatively affect the successful implementation of organizational functions and responsibilities.

Furthermore, managers also lack ability to use concrete evidence to provide appropriate and acceptable decisions. Out of the total respondents 48 (44.4%) of Gindeberet woreda and 32 (50.8%) of Abuna Gindeberet woreda respondents graded the ability of their managers to make use of concrete evidence as low and satisfactory respectively. Moreover, 42 (38.9%) and 29 (46%) of Gindeberet and Abuna Gindeberet woreda valued the ability of their managers to use concrete evidence and provide acceptable decision as satisfactory and low respectively while the rest of 18 (16.7%) of the former woreda and 2 (3.2%) of the later woreda replied as high. It seems that managers of Abuna Gindeberet woreda are better off than Gindeberet woreda in making use of concrete evidences to provide decision. Such form of evidence based decisions enhances the acceptability of the decision and, if not all, it satisfies most parties.

In addition, employees were requested to evaluate whether their managers made efforts to set standards, goals and objectives for performance and 57 (52.7%) of Gindeberet woreda and 37 (58.7%) of Abuna Gindeberet woreda respondents answered as reasonable. Moreover, 33.3 percent of respondents of both woredas indicated the extent of managers effort to set standards and benchmarks for performance as low while the rest of 15 (13.9%) of former woreda and 5 (7.9%) of the later woreda respondents ranked the ability of their managers to set standards, goals, and objectives for performance as great. This implies how far managers lack competence to set standards and benchmarks to improve the planning and implementation capacities of woreda's public sectors that in turn enable measure the success and failures of the set targets and objectives.

Accurate information provided through a system of top-down flows and feedback is vital to keep employees aware about what needs to be done, and to keep managers informed about what was achieved. Apart from the specific information needed to carry out work, it also helps to motivate employees of an organization making them feel they are part of an important effort and a wider purpose. However, the survey result revealed that managers of different levels lack communication skills. Out of the total respondents, 55 (50.9) of Gindeberet woreda and 31 (49.2%) of Abuna Gindeberet woreda respondents specified the communication skill of their managers as acceptable while 46 (42.6%) of the former woreda and 27 (42.9%) of the later woreda respondents valued their managers communication skills as high. Therefore, this lack of managers' communication skills results into lack of mutual interaction, exchange of information, cooperation, that in turn bring about huge gaps that negatively affect the performance of work as employees and managers are not aware of each other and do not have up to date information about the changes going on. This could be demonstrated through lack of cooperation and interaction between employee and managers. In this regard, 51 (47.2%) of Gindeberet woreda and 32 (50.8%) of Abuna Gindeberet woreda respondents evaluated the cooperative abilities of their managers as satisfactory while the rest of 49 (45.4%) of the earlier woreda and 26 (41.3%) of the later woreda respondents rated the cooperative abilities of their managers as low. Moreover, 8 (7.4%) of Gindeberet woreda and 5 (7.9%) of Abuna Gindeberet woreda respondents regarded the cooperative ability of their managers as high.

It seems sound to delegate authority whenever someone is unable to engage into their regular work, however, the survey result shows the reverse as 55 (50.9%) of Gindeberet woreda and 33 (52.4%) of Abuna Gindeberet woreda respondents rated the ability of managers to delegate authority as insignificant whereas 34 (31.5%) of the prior woreda and 26 (41.3%) of the later woreda evaluated the ability of their managers to delegate authority and responsibility whenever appropriate as acceptable. Moreover, 19 (17.6%) of Gindeberet woreda and 4 (6.3%) of Abuna Gindeberet woreda respondents answered as high. Therefore, it appears that managers of Gindeberet woreda are well positioned to delegate authority and responsibility whenever appropriate than Abuna Gindeberet woredas.

Moreover, employees were requested to rate the extent to which managers provide decisions that are participatory providing an opportunity for more diverse and complete information, and increase the legitimacy and acceptance of the proposed course of action. However, the result of the survey reveals the reverse as 50 (46.3%) of Gindeberet woreda respondents and 33 (52.4%) of Abuna Gindeberet woreda respondents rated the extent to which managers provide participatory decision as acceptable and negligible respectively whereas 48 (44.4%) of Gindeberet woreda and 26 (41.3%) of Abuna Gindeberet woreda respondents answered as low and satisfactory respectively. Further, 10 (9.3%) of Gindeberet woreda and 4 (6.3%) of Abuna Gindeberet woreda respondents replied as high to the same issue. Here, it is important to mention that Gindeberet woreda constitute a better experience of providing participatory decision though it needs to work much on it to farther it. Accordingly, such non-participatory decisions may result into decisions that are unacceptable in the eyes of other parties as decision making processes are constrained by limits to decision-makers' information processing capacity, as well as their background, position in the organization, interests, and experiences. Therefore, it is important to consider decisions that are participatory and inclusive.

In order for decentralization to achieve the intended goal the role of competent, skilled and qualified human resource is critical, and the realization of this effort largely depends on the role of managers. However, contrary to this fact 63 (58.3%) of Gindeberet woreda respondents and 37 (58.7%) of Abuna Gindeberet woreda respondents ranked the effort of managers to develop human resources as low while 36 (33.3%) of Gindeberet wereda and 19 (30.2%) of Abuna Gindeberet woreda respondents evaluated the efforts of managers to build the human capacity of the organization as satisfactory. Moreover, the remaining 9 (8.3%) of Gindeberet woreda and 7 (11.1%) of Abuna Gindeberet woreda respondents rated the effort of managers to build human capacity as high.

It is widely held view that one of the rationales for decentralization is to improve the competitiveness of governments and enhance innovation and creativity in order to satisfy the wishes of citizens. Decentralization could allow all three governance institutions (government, the private sector, and civil society organizations) to become more creative and innovative in responding to public needs. Accordingly, respondents were requested whether their managers have creativity and innovativeness, and 75 (69.4%) of Gindeberet woreda and 49 (77.8%) of Abuna Gindeberet woreda respondents replied as insignificant or low. Moreover, 30 (27.8%) of the prior woreda and 13 (20.6%) of Abuna Gindeberet woreda respondents uncovered the reasonable level of the creativity and innovativeness of their respective managers while the remaining 3 (2.8%) and 1 (1.6%) of the former and the later woreda exposed the creativity and innovativeness of their managers as high.

Moreover, the survey result about managers' knowledge of current trends in organizational governance reveals that managers have critical knowledge gap of the current trends in organizational governance. In this regard, out of the total sample size requested to rate managers knowledge of current trends in organizational governance 63 (58.3%) of Gindeberet woreda and 37 (58.7%) of Abuna Gindeberet woreda respondents rated their managers knowledge of the current trends in organizational governance as low whereas 36 (33.3%) of the former woreda and 22 (34.9%) of Abuna Gindeberet woreda respondents rated the same issue as satisfactory while the rest of 9 (8.3%) and 4 (6.3%) of Gindeberet and Abuna Gindeberet woredas respondents respectively evaluated the knowledge of managers as high. Such type of managerial knowledge gaps would create inflexibility and inadaptability to the flux and rapidly changing environment which in turn results into the stagnation of the organization which finally leads to complete failure.

Furthermore, employees were requested to rate the ability of their managers to set acceptable organizational strategy, and 55 (50.9%) of Gindeberet woreda respondents and 30 (47.6%) of Abuna Gindeberet woreda respondents evaluated the capacity of their managers to set acceptable organizational strategy as satisfactory while 47 (43.5%) of former woreda respondents and 30 (47.6%) of Abuna Gindeberet woreda respondents rated the same issue as low. Moreover, the remaining 6 (5.6%) of Gindeberet woreda and 3 (4.8%) of Abuna Gindeberet woreda respondents replied as high.

3.2.4. Financial Capacity

Lack of resources implies incapacity of any agency. Accordingly, financial responsibility is at the core of the concept of decentralization as it is the most important determinant resource to the successful implementations of decentralization. Evidences reveal that in most developing countries decentralization policies have been plagued by financial deficiencies that would pose difficulty on local governments of covering their basic operating expenses, training their personnel, purchasing equipment, making organizational improvements, obtaining technical assistance, and expanding the range and quality of public services (Rondinelli et.al., 1983; Shah, 1999). In this regard, the decentralization policy of Ethiopia is not an exception as different levels of governments suffered from lack of sufficient financial capacity to finance their decentralized responsibilities and functions (Mehret, 2002; Tegegne and Kassahun, 2004; Dickovick and Tegegne, 2010). It is worth noting, however, that for decentralization to work local government must have adequate financial resources, usually from a combination of local revenues and grants from central government. Hence, if decentralization is to have an impact on enabling local organizations to provide services and infrastructure more effectively, local organizations must have stronger authority to raise revenues and generate large amounts of revenues.

Realizing this, the government has designed two strategies to alleviate the problem. These strategies were region-woreda fiscal transfer and own revenue generation through allocation of financial resources required for local development on efficacy and equity basis by introducing credible, transparent and fair region-woreda transfer formula, and enhance the capacity and incentives of woreda for mobilizing own revenues and use of funds respectively. Accordingly, the Oromia National Regional State has revised the been providing block grants which is by and large a general purpose grant to woreda, town and zonal administration based on their expenditure obligation and affordable needs, conditioned to bring about measurable outcomes even though there are some ongoing projects and non-discretionary payments such as salary, which forcefully divert the grant to predefined purpose to be qualified as specific purpose grant.

An official document, Local Governments Block Grant Allocation Formula, shows that the regional government has its own formula and criteria on the basis of which it provides grants to woredas. In this regard, the previous formula provides 55% weight for population index, 30% for development index and 15% for revenue index. However, it is a capital biased and it was designed to measure the relative capital needs of the woredas. The variables included in the formula are those variables, which measure the infrastructure deficit of the woredas with respect to their population. Therefore, it doesn't measure the actual budgetary needs of the woredas. It also includes variables out of the domain of expenditure obligation of the woredas such as telephone and electricity indices. The policy variables included in the formula are packed together in such a way that is difficult to manipulate as per the requirement of the regional development policies and strategies. The weighting of the variables is also too subjective and has no relationship with government priorities and objective realities. In general the formula has the following limitations that includes it doesn't explicitly show the relation between financial performance with government policies, goals and objectives, doesn't measure recurrent needs, gives less emphasis for other than population, doesn't favor efficient and equitable utilization of resource, and provides subjective weighting.

As a result, following the inauguration of District Level Decentralization Program the new formula which was based on the fundamental principles of efficiency, equity, adequacy and comprehensiveness, transparency and comprehensibility, and stability and predictability came into being in 2002/2003. The very ideas of the new need based, outcome conditional and general-purpose grant are to address on the minimum the basic needs in terms of existing commitment and sustainable service expansion for the steady growth of service needs, to give discretion for woredas in their financial management in order to foster their creative engagement and bring about measurable results. This block grant force woredas to set their goals, objectives and priorities as per the priorities and targets of the regional government. It mainly takes into considerations the development sector and socio-economic activities. The grant mainly focuses on the five strategic sectors or poverty reduction sectors (education, health, agriculture and rural development, water, and roads). The Block grant calculation establishes a recurrent-capital ratio of 73:27. However, the short comings of this formula is that it is not established by empirical study but by expert opinion and past experiences backed by the decision of higher officials. Moreover, the formula falls short of the participation of the main stakeholders and engine of development, woredas, as only zonal, special woredas and regional government officials are part of the enactment of the formula.

Woreda officials and woreda Office of Finance and Economic Development officials were asked about whether finances as provided in the budget are released timely, awareness of the criteria used to apportion the budget (block grant), whether the formula enables appropriate allocation of resources, the adequacy of power and autonomy to decide on the block grant budget, and the happiness with the budget formula and the amount of money the woreda get. According to Table 3, woredas have limited autonomy and discretion to set priorities and targets as 11 out of 15 respondents in Gindeberet woreda and 5 out of 7 respondents in Abuna Gindeberet woreda rated their autonomy to set priorities and targets as satisfactory whereas 4 and 1 respondents of Gindeberet and Abuna Gindeberet woredas respectively replied as high.

Moreover, respondents were asked the extent to which the regional government consult woredas while deciding the budget, and 9 of Gindeberet woreda respondents and 4 of Abuna Gindeberet woreda respondents indicated the reasonable level to which the regional government consult the woreda under study while deciding on the budget whereas 4 of the earlier woreda respondents and 3 of the later woreda respondents revealed the extent to which regional government consult woredas as low.

According to the survey result (Table 3), 10 out of 15 respondents and 3 of Gindeberet and Abuna Gindeberet woreda respondents respectively indicated whether budget are released timely as satisfactory whereas 3 of the former woreda and 2 of the later woreda respondents rated the same issue as low. Moreover, 2 respondents of Gindeberet and Abuna Gindeberet woreda respondents replied whether budgets are released timely as high.

Furthermore, the formula used to apportion the block grant should be simple, understandable, transparent, and be based on objective criteria to reduce ambiguity. In this regard, woreda officials were asked the extent to which they are aware of the criteria used to allocate the budget, and 6 and 4 of Gindeberet woreda and Abuna Gindeberet woreda respondents respectively specified that they lack awareness whereas 6 and 3 of the former woreda and the later woreda respondents respectively demonstrated that they are aware of the criteria to a reasonable degree. Moreover, it seems that Gindeberet woreda officials were more aware of the criteria used to apportion the budget as 3 out of 15 respondents answered as high.

Besides, officials were also asked the level to which the formula enables appropriate allocation of resources, and 8 of Gindeberet woreda and 4 of Abuna Gindeberet woreda respondents made known that they do not think that the formula enables appropriate allocation of resources while 5 of the former woreda respondents and 3 of the later woreda respondents showed that the formula would enable proper allocation of resources. In light of this, the survey result demonstrated that woredas were not happy/ satisfied with the budget formula and the money they get as 9 of Gindeberet woreda and 4 of Abuna Gindeberet woreda respondents replied their dissatisfaction to the formula. Whereas, 5 of the earlier woreda and 3 of the later woreda rated the happiness they drive from the budget formula as acceptable.

Whatever the response of the officials might be the regional government has been providing woredas with budget. For instance in 2009/2010 fiscal year out of the total budget allocated to Gindeberet and Abuna Gindeberet woredas the grant covers 80.5 and 85.7 percent respectively while the remaining 19.5 and 14.3 percent of woreda activities were to be financed by the revenue generated by woredas themselves. In the same token, in the year 2010/2011 and 2011/2012 similar trends have been manifested as woredas rely on regional governments for more than 80 percent of their total budget. This fact and figures can be indicated in table 4 below:

Table 4: Budget and Sources of Budget in Gindeberet and Abuna Gindeberet Woredas

Budget	**Fiscal Years**					
	Gindeberet Woreda			**Abuna Gindeberet Woreda**		
	2009/10	**2010/11**	**2011/12**	**2009/10**	**2010/11**	**2011/12**
Recurrent Budget	15,129,179	18,786,968	27,266,165	14,809,782	17,924,297	26,404,224
Capital Budget	1,064,236	1,600,583	2,361,476	1,015,387	1,961,845	2,302,167
Miscellaneous	1,22,497	131,858	142,512	80,000	100,000	100,000
Total	**16,315,912**	**20,519,409**	**29,803,153**	**15,905,169**	**19,986,142**	**28,806,391**
Sources of Budget						
Woreda Tax-revenue	2,307,472.38	2,483,740	4,148,183	150,000	160,000	2,390,000
Woreda non-tax revenue	870,652.62	699,064	1,732,640	2,122,412	3,006,341	1,945,902
Total Woreda Revenue	**3,178,125**	**3,182,804**	**5,880,823**	**2,272,412**	**3,166,341**	**4,335,902**
Regional government block grant	13,137,792	17,336,605	24,290,330	13,632,757	16,819,801	24,470,489

Source: Gindeberet and Abuna Gindeberet Woredas Finance and Economic Development Office

A closer look at the table above discloses that woredas are awfully dependent on the grant they gain from the regional government as the revenue collected by woredas is insignificant to finance their decentralized responsibilities and functions properly. In order to get information about the ability of the woredas to generate own revenue, and the existence of diversified sources of revenue questionnaires was administered to woreda officials and woreda Finance and Economic Development officials (see table 3 above). Accordingly, concerning the ability of the woredas to generate their own revenue, out of the total sample size 7 (46.7%) of Gindeberet woreda and 5 (71.4%) of Abuna Gindeberet woreda indicated the inadequacy of the ability of the woreda to generate revenue whereas 6 (40%) of the earlier woreda and 2 (28.6%) of the later woreda revealed the acceptable ability of woredas to generate their own revenue. The remaining 2 (13.3%) of Gindeberet woreda respondents specified the greater ability of the woreda to generate its own revenue. Accordingly, it seems that Gindeberet woreda is better off in its capacity to generate revenue. The limited ability to generate revenue is caused by both internal as well as external factors that impedes the revenue generating effort of woredas. Internal factors include, lack of enough space/offices, lack of budget, lack of trainings to enhance and improve the implementing capacity of experts and managers, and lack of human resource capacity. External aspects influencing the revenue generating capacity of woredas are lack of timeliness due to lack of awareness among the community about the benefits of revenue and taxes, the influence of the topography, lack of transport services, the merger of revenue collection with Oromia Development Association, Red Cross, and income from sport have reduced the revenue that should be collected from rural land administration, lack of proper control by the office of trade that contributed to the proliferation of illegal businesses, and tax evasion.

With regard to the sources of the revenue, 11 (73.3%) of Gindeberet woreda and 4 (57.1%) of Abuna Gindeberet woreda respondents showed the presence of low sources of revenue while 4 (26.7%) of earlier woreda and 3 (42.9%) of the later woreda disclosed the existence of adequate sources of revenue respectively.

A society's capacity to meet the needs of its members depends not only on the resources available to it, but it largely relies on how best those resources are utilized. A good financial management and sound financial management would inspire funders and enables create confidence in them. To this end, the availability of adequate and qualified human resources that undertake this activity is important to achieve the intended objective. Accordingly, respondents were asked the adequacy of available human resources to ensure a good financial control and information system, and 8 (53.3%) of Gindeberet woreda respondents and 4 (57.1%) of Abuna Gindeberet woreda respondents indicated the availability of adequate and low human resources to ensure a good financial control and information system respectively. Moreover, 6 (40%) of earlier woreda and 4 (57.1%) of the later woreda mentioned the availability of adequate and insufficient human resources to ensure financial management.

Furthermore, respondents were asked whether auditors of the organization are happy with the controls of cash and assets being utilized, and 8 (53.3%) of Gindeberet woreda and 4 (57.1%) of

Abuna Gindeberet woreda replied as low and satisfactory respectively while the remaining 7 (46.7%) of the former woreda and 4 (57.1%) of the later woreda rated the same issue as low and satisfactory consecutively. Besides, the focus group discussions illustrate the unavailability of adequate and competent human resources to ensure good financial management and assets. This is mainly due to the absence of structure that offers internal auditors and lack of budget to hire skilled and competent staffs.

Moreover, woredas spent more than 90 percent of their budget to recurrent expenditure which focuses on expansion of the existing services and used for salary and operational expenses whereas the remaining less than 10 percent is spent for capital expenditures. For example, out of the total budget allocated to Gindeberet woreda in three consecutive fiscal years recurrent budget constitute 15,129,179, 18,786,968, and 27,266,165 which is more than 90% of total budget. The same holds true for Abuna Gindeberet woreda. This shows the degree to which local governments focus on expanding the already existing services.

3.2.5. Availability of Facilities

The limited physical infrastructure, transport and communications facilities, restricted access to services and facilities in rural areas hinders interaction among local communities, district and provincial governments, and between them and the central government too (Rondinelli, et.al., 1983). Decentralized units also found it hard to interact with each other or to coordinate their activities within regions. Considering this the Ethiopian government has designed a strategy under District Level Decentralization Program that aimed at enhancing and improving the infrastructure and office equipment. It aimed at creating enabling working environment by strengthening disadvantaged rural woredas and woreda offices with basic office equipment, ICT and related office facilities. However, the survey result demonstrated little attention has been given in the design and implementation of decentralization policies to the impacts of infrastructure and office facilities in Gindeberet and Abuna Gindeberet woredas.

If one takes a closer look at Table 5 above, relatively except computer service and offices which are on better position, the other office facilities are almost unavailable. For instance, respondents were requested to rate the accessibility of telephone services, and 88 (81.5%) of Gindeberet woreda respondents and 51 (81%) of Abuna Gindeberet woreda respondents rated the availability of telephone service as negligible whereas the rest of 19 (17.6%) of earlier woreda and 10 (15.9%) of the later woreda specified as satisfactory. Moreover, 1 (0.9%) of Gindeberet woreda and 2 (3.2%) of Abuna Gindeberet woreda respondents answered the availability of telephone service as high. Besides, personal experience reveals not only the inadequacy of telephone services in different local government offices and departments but also the unavailability of telephone services in the locality at all. Even though telephone line was already stretched in Gindeberet woreda in 2006, due to technical problems the service was detached since 2002 E.C. while Abuna Gindeberet woreda make use of wireless telephone services.

With regards to the availability of vehicle services, 106 (98.1%) of Gindeberet woreda respondents and 60 (95.2%) of Abuna Gindeberet woreda respondents evaluated its accessibility as low while the remaining 2 (1.9%) of earlier woreda and 3 (4.8%) of Abuna Gindeberet woreda respondents revealed the adequacy of vehicle services. Moreover, the availability of computer service was stated by 64 (59.3%) and 50 (79.4%) of respondents of Gindeberet and Abuna Gindeberet woreda consecutively as insignificant while 4 (3.7%) and 40 (37%) of Gindeberet woreda and 1 (1.6%) and 12 (19%) of Abuna Gindeberet woreda rated the accessibility of computer services as high and satisfactory respectively.

Internet service is one of the most important tools that facilitate communication both internally and externally as well as enables acquire updated information about the ever changing world. However, contrary to the plan of the government, ICT services like internet is almost unavailable except on mobile phone in the study woredas. This observation can be justified by the survey results, as 106 (98.1%) of Gindeberet woreda respondents and 61 (96.8%) of Abuna Gindeberet woreda respondents rated the availability of internet services as low whereas the remaining 1 (0.9%) of earlier woreda and 2 (3.2%) of Abuna Gindeberet woreda respondents rated satisfactory. As far as computer networking is concerned, 97 (89.8%) of Gindeberet woreda and 61 (96.8%) of Abuna Gindeberet woreda respondents ranked as low while the rest of 9 (8.3%) of former woreda and 2 (3.2%) of the later woreda graded the accessibility of computer networking as adequate.

The processes by which information is decoded, processed, and stored underlie most local government functions. The available local government data has to be reliable, accurate and consistent. To this end, the existence of appropriate databases and filing systems is essential for instance to the ability to collect taxes, as well rapid socio-economic transformation is unthinkable without accurate and reliable data. Accordingly, this survey has tried to assess the availability of strong database in Gindeberet and Abuna Gindeberet woredas however, the result showed almost the non-existence of strong database in both woredas as 96 (88.9%) of Gindeberet woreda and 55 (81.3%) of Abuna Gindeberet woreda respondents replied as low while the remaining 12 (11.1%) and 11 (18.7%) of Gindeberet and Abuna Gindeberet woreda respondents indicated the presence of adequate database respectively. This shows that the woreda has weak and poor data recording systems that deteriorate the existence of reliable and valid data that demonstrates the reality in the woredas under study.

Moreover, the existence of adequate buildings and infrastructures to run the day to day activities of offices play a paramount role to effectively discharge local governments' constitutional mandates and responsibilities. Accordingly, employees of the two woredas were asked whether adequate buildings and offices are there, and 75 (69.4%) and 47 (74.6%) of Gindeberet and Abuna Gindeberet woreda respondents respectively stated the inadequacy of available offices to discharge their day to day activities. Moreover, 32 (29.6%) of Gindeberet woreda respondents and 14 (22.2%) of Abuna Gindeberet woreda respondents exhibited the adequacy of buildings and infrastructures while the remaining 1 (0.9%) of the former woreda and 2 (3.2%) of the later woreda respondents answered the same issue as high. Personal observation also reveals that the problem is more acute in Abuna Gindeberet woreda as two or more sector offices are forced to work under the same roof, the ground is full of dust, and do not have ceilings.

3.2.6. Enabling Work Environment

Each organization is set in a particular environment to which it is closely linked. This environment provides multiple contexts that affect the organization and its performance, what it produces, and how it operates. Enabling environments support effective and efficient organizations and individuals, and creating such environments is becoming an increasingly important aspect of capacity development. The concept of an enabling environment is the key to understanding and explaining the forces that help shape the character and performance of organizations. Therefore, any effort to analyze and improve the performance of an organization requires an understanding of the forces inside and outside the organization that can facilitate or inhibit that performance.

3.2.6.1. Internal Enabling Environment

Factors that make up the internal environment include the organization's culture, performance related incentive and rewards, the history and traditions of the organization, leadership and management style, the existence of a generally recognized and accepted mission statement, organizational structure (division of labor and definition of roles, responsibilities, and authority), and shared norms and values.

Although District Level Decentralization Program intended to improve and enhance woreda working systems for planning and implementation and service delivery, the survey revealed that the overall internal environment of the local government is weak. This could be demonstrated through different factors. For instance, it is obvious that the existence of proper organizational structure is crucial to the coordination and integration of different activities. Moreover, the clarity and simplicity of the structures and procedures used to decentralize, the ability of the implementing agency staff to interact with higher level authorities, and the extent to which components of decentralized programs are integrated influences the outcomes of decentralization efforts. In light of this, employees were asked whether there is appropriate structure for key functions, and 71 (65.7%) of Gindeberet woreda and 32 (50.8%) of Abuna Gindeberet woreda respondents illustrated the presence of structure to address key functions as low. Moreover, 35 (31.5%) of Gindeberet woreda and 27 (42.9%) of Abuna Gindeberet woreda respondents replied as satisfactory to the same question while the remaining 3 (2.8%) of Gindeberet woreda and 4 (6.3%) of Abuna Gindeberet woreda respondents ranked the existence of appropriate structure for key functions in their respective office as high. Hence, lack of appropriate organizational structures and procedures hinders the effort of staffs to meet their obligations, including development of a good working relationship with officials, among staffs themselves, and elected representative councils as well as inappropriately designed and implemented structures and processes will lead to the failure of decentralization.

Furthermore, the survey result showed lack of clear and stable structures and systems to be followed in the study areas. With this regard, 75 (69.4%) of Gindeberet woreda respondents and 37 (58.7%) of Abuna Gindeberet woreda respondents demonstrated the prevalence of relatively unstable and unclear structures and systems while the remaining 28 (25.9%) and 26 (41.3%) of the same woreda respectively indicated the presence of acceptable level of stable and clear organizational structure. Moreover, it seems that Gindeberet woreda has more clear and stable structure than Abuna Gindeberet woreda as 5 (4.6%) of respondents of Gindeberet woreda exhibited the presence of high degree of clear and stable work structure whereas none in Abuna Gindeberet woreda. The ever changing work structure have created difficulty to workers to stay stable and committed to the position they held which in turn negatively affected the performance of job and the effective implementation of the plan.

Moreover, the respondents were asked whether employees understand the objectives of the organization and 68 (63%) of Gindeberet woreda and 36 (57.1%) of Abuna Gindeberet woreda respondents replied that employee understand the objectives of their respective offices to a reasonable level. In addition, 32 (29.6%) of Gindeberet woreda and 22 (34.9%) of Abuna Gindeberet woreda respondents disclosed the low level of awareness of objectives of offices while the remaining 8 (7.4%) of the former woreda and 5 (7.9%) of the later woreda argued the existence of high degree of awareness of the objectives of offices among employee. Furthermore, line of authority is not well understood in local governments under study as 66 (61.1%) and 39 (61.9%) of the respondents in Gindeberet and Abuna Gindeberet woredas respectively responded as low while 38 (35.2%) of Gindeberet woreda respondents and 21 (33.3%) of Abuna Gindeberet woreda respondents exhibited as satisfactory. Besides, 4 (3.7%) of the earlier woreda and 3 (4.8%) of the later woreda indicated the high degree of understanding of line of authority among employee. This low degree of awareness of objectives and the existence of unclear line of authority poses difficulty on measuring the proper implementation, monitoring and evaluation of plans and development activities as there is weak chain of check and balance.

Capacity building involves beyond enhancing knowledge and skills of individuals. It largely depends on the quality of the organizations in which individuals work. The operation of particular organization in turn relies on the enabling environment i.e. the structure of power and influence and the institutions in which they are embedded. With this regard, employees were asked whether there is conducive working conditions that stimulate employee to be committed to their work, and 83 (76.9%) of Gindeberet woreda and 44 (69.3%) of Abuna Gindeberet woreda indicated the existence of limited inspiring work situation while the remaining 21 (19.4%) and 19 (30.2%) of respondents of the same woreda respectively argued the presence of tolerable amount of good working environment. Here, it is important to mention that Gindeberet woreda has relatively more conducive working condition than Abuna Gindeberet woreda as 4 (3.7%) of respondents indicated the presence of highly conducive working situation.

Capacity is not only about skills and procedures; it is also about incentives as an organization's competitiveness depends in part on its ability to create an environment that motivates and stimulates its personnel, and it is highly likely that staff who are reasonably comfortable with working conditions and stimulated by the environment will be productive. The assessment and reward system helps the organization to retain good employees, motivate staff, facilitate organizational strategic objectives, and support individual learning. In connection with this, 107 (99.1%) employee of Gindeberet woreda and 57 (90.5%) of Abuna Gindeberet woreda exposed the unavailability of employee recognition programs such as incentives, rewards, promotion, etc. for good performance while the remaining 1 (0.9%) of former woreda and 6 (9.8%) of the later woreda respondents specified the existence of acceptable level of employee recognition programs. Similarly, the study has showed the unavailability of employee recognition since BPR came into force as there was no system of evaluation of employee performance upon which promotions, incentives, and rewards were to be provided. As a result, the absence of such system has increased employee turnover, discouraged employee performance and commitment to work as the every employee was on the same rank.

Besides, it is clearly seen in Table 6 above that 85 (78.7%) of employee of Gindeberet woreda and 53 (84.1%) of employee of Abuna Gindeberet woreda uncovered that key positions are not adequately filled while the remaining 13 (12%) and 9 (14.3%) of both woreda respondents respectively proved that key positions are filled. Lack of sufficient budget, ever expanding and changing organizational work structure, etc. are identified as responsible for key positions not to be filled adequately. Moreover, respondents were asked whether regular meetings were held among members of staff and 64 (59.3%) of Gindeberet woreda respondents and 37 (58.7%) of Abuna Gindeberet woreda respondents specified the limited availability of meetings among staffs whereas 44 (40.7%) and 26 (41.3%) of both woredas respectively implied the availability of regular meetings. This lack of regular meetings could negatively affect the performance of job as employees are not informed about new issues, changes and progresses in the organizations to adapt and coup up with the changes.

Most importantly, as far as the monitoring and evaluation capacity of local governments under study are concerned, 51 (47.2%) of Gindeberet woreda respondents and 34 (54%) of Abuna Gindeberet woreda respondents referred the presence of strong and weak monitoring and evaluation systems respectively in their respective woredas while the rest of 57 (52.8%) of the former woreda and 28 (44.4%) of Abuna Gindeberet woreda respondents indicated the existence of weak and strong monitoring and evaluation systems in their respective woredas. This situation reveals the relative strength of monitoring and evaluation system in Abuna Gindeberet woreda than that of Gindeberet woreda.

Rules, directives, laws and guidelines must be written concisely and describe clearly and simply, the relationships and obligations of officials and citizens, the allocation of functions among units, and the roles and duties of leaders at each level as well as the relationship among employee and their duties and responsibilities. In this regard respondents were requested to comment whether there are clear rules, directives and guidelines for employees, and 64 (59.3%) of respondents of Gindeberet woreda and 31 (49.2%) of Abuna Gindeberet woreda respondents indicated the presence of lack of clear rules and regulation to guide employee. Moreover, 43 (39.8%) of Gindeberet woreda respondents and 31 (49.2%) of Abuna Gindeberet woreda answered the availability of directives and procedures to guide employee while the remaining respondents replied that they are not aware of such situation at all.

A society's capacity to meet the needs of its members depends on the resources available to it, and largely on how best those resources are utilized. Accordingly, management of an organization's financial resources and other asset is a critical capacity. Good management of finance is essential to the overall functioning of the organization inspiring confidence in funders interested in financial accountability and sound financial management. Accordingly, respondents were asked whether the financial management of the office is weak, and 56 (51.9%) of Gindeberet woreda respondents, and 32 (50.8%) of Abuna Gindeberet woreda respondents exhibited the availability of strong and weak financial management respectively. Moreover, 47 (43.5%) of Gindeberet woreda and 46 (29%) of Abuna Gindeberet woreda respondents ascertained the availability of weak and strong financial management system. This shows that Gindeberet woreda is relatively better than Abuna Gindeberet woreda in terms of financial management. According to the focus group discussion, weak financial management is resulted from lack of adequate and qualified human resources to monitor and evaluate the financial management. Moreover, the absence of internal auditors to each sectoral office since the existing organizational structure of woreda offices does not offer the position. Besides, the participant to the focus group discussion ascertained the unavailability of assets management.

The cumulated impact of the above mentioned drawbacks and problems is reflected in the inability of different sector offices to effectively implement or execute their plans and achieve their objectives. In this regard, respondents were asked whether their respective offices execute their plans as intended, and 69 (63.9%) of Gindeberet woreda respondents and 35 (55.6%) of Abuna Gindeberet woreda respondents answered the failure of their sector offices to achieve their plan whereas 35 (32.4%) of the former woreda and 27 (42.9%) of the later woreda respondents answered that plans are implemented as intended. But the remaining percent of respondents responded that they are not informed whether plans are executed as intended. The focus group discussion with officials of both woredas specified, in addition to the above mentioned factors, lack of being informed and aware as well as lack of accepting the plan, overload of jobs, and the participation of employee on different jobs beside their area of concern are identified as causes that hindered the effective implementation of plans in the study woredas.

3.2.6.2. External Enabling Environment

The external environment in which the organization operates also has a strong influence on the performance of an organization. These factors that make up external working environment comprises of administrative and legal systems that govern the organization, the political environment, and the social and cultural context in which the organization operates. In this regard, most of respondents explained that the overall external enabling environment of both woredas is not conducive to work. For instance, respondents were requested to rate whether laws and procedures regarding powers and duties of woredas are clearly communicated except the constitution, and 59 (54.6%) of Gindeberet woreda and 30 (47.6%) of Abuna Gindeberet woreda respondents indicated the presence of lack of such trends of communication of laws and procedures regarding duties and powers of woreda except the constitution. Moreover, 29 (26.9%) of Gindeberet woreda and 26 (41.3%) of Abuna Gindeberet woreda respondents uncovered the availability of trends of communicating laws and procedures regarding powers and duties of woreda except the constitution whereas the rest of 20 (18.5%) and 7 (11.1%) of Gindeberet and Abuna Gindeberet woreda respondents respectively clarified that they are not even aware of anything about the issue raised. In connection with this issue it is noted from the focus group discussion that previously sectoral offices were responsible to make aware employee of their own their rights and responsibilities and such activity was very rare however, since 2003E.C. the mandate was relocated to woreda Civil Service and Good Governance Office, and since then there is a good beginning to offer short term trainings to the entire employees about their right and duties.

It is widely shared view that an individuals, organizations, or institutions that do not have a vision do not know where to go, what to do and for whom to do. This shows the extent to which setting and understanding vision is important to the successful accomplishment of one's mission and goals. Decentralization as a policy has its own rationales and goals to be attained while it was implemented at national, regional, and local levels. Accordingly, for the goal of decentralization to be achieved it has paramount importance to understand and recognize its vision. In this regard, respondents were asked the degree to which local level actors (public, private, civil society organizations, etc.) have clear vision over the goal of decentralization, and 63 (58.3%) of Gindeberet woreda respondents and 30 (47.6%) of Abuna Gindeberet woreda respondents designated the low degree of awareness about the vision of decentralization. Further, 29 (26.9%) and 31 (42.1%) of Gindeberet and Abuna Gindeberet woreda respondents referred that local level stakeholders have clear vision of decentralization while the remaining 16 (14.8%) and 2 (3.2%) of Gindeberet woreda and Abuna Gindeberet woreda respondents respectively proved that they are not informed about the issue raised.

There is fairly widespread agreement that capacity building at all government levels is an essential component of decentralization. It is argued that capacity building enhances the degree of the effectiveness of decentralization policies at different level. Accordingly, the Ethiopia government has executed capacity building initiatives with an intention to enhance the ability of different tiers of government to effectively implement their mandates and responsibilities. As a result, in order to evaluate the degree to which capacity building policy enhanced decentralization process in the locality, respondents were asked whether the effort of capacity building improved the decentralization process in the locality, and 69 (63.9%) of Gindeberet woreda and 34 (54%) of Abuna Gindeberet woreda respondents explained that the effort of capacity building has brought about negligible changes or improvements to decentralization whereas 24 (22.2%) of Gindeberet woreda and 26 (41.3%) of Abuna Gindeberet woreda implied that the effort of capacity building have brought about significant and concrete improvement to decentralization. Moreover, the remaining 15 (13.9%) of Gindeberet woreda and 3 (4.8%) of Abuna Gindeberet woreda respondents explained that they are not aware of the issue at all. However, opposite to this fact, the regional bureau officials revealed that the capacity building initiative has highly improved decentralized system of governance.

It is obvious that coordination and communication among different level of government and among different stakeholders facilitates and enhance the degree of shared experience. Accordingly, the respondents were requested to grade the degree of horizontal coordination in the local government, as a result 58 (53.7%) of Gindeberet woreda and 32 (50.8%) of Abuna Gindeberet woreda respondents unveiled that such type of coordination is almost unavailable and fragile whereas 29 (26.9%) of former woreda and 24 (38.1%) of the later woreda respondents disclosed the existence of substantial degree of horizontal coordination in the local government. Moreover, the remaining 21 (19.4%) and 7 (11.1%) of Gindeberet and Abuna Gindeberet woreda respondents respectively explained that they are not informed about the situation at all. However, contrary to this fact interview with bureau official revealed the high level of coordination among woredas.

Moreover, it is important for local level actors and institutions to undertake SWOT analysis about their working conditions in order to ensure their survival. Accordingly, respondents were asked whether sectors or offices recognize and understand their current strength, weakness, opportunities and threats and 43 (39.8%) of Gindeberet woreda and 38 (60.3%) of Abuna Gindeberet woreda responded as no and Yes respectively while 42 (38.9%) of former woreda and 23 (36.5%) of later woreda responded the availability and non-availability of SWOT analysis in their respective sector offices. Surprisingly the remaining respondents answered that they are not informed of such issues at all. Similarly, the focus group discussion also uncovered that though SWOT analysis was undertaken during planning period, majority of employees were not informed about the strength and weakness of their offices as planning was conducted by limited individuals who hold the leadership position.

Besides, in order to strengthen the capacity of local governments' regional governments should play a facilitatory role and they should create an enabling environment under which local government operates. Such roles could be undertaken through provision of various resources such as facilities, funds, human resources, etc. as well as through preparation of different directives, guidelines, rules and regulations that further support and strengthen local governments. However, the survey result specified that the support from the regional government is insignificant as 94 (87%) of Gindeberet woreda and 53 (84.1%) of Abuna Gindeberet woreda respondents unveiled the support from the regional government is not as such reasonable while 8

(7.4%) of the former woreda and 9 (14.3%) of the later woreda respondents replied that the regional government is making a significant backing to local governments under study. Moreover, the remaining respondents argued that they do not know what is going on in connection with this issue.

3.2.7. Community Participation

Community participation is considered as an essential part of successful decentralization as decentralized decision making enlarges possibilities for local participation in development. Citizen oversight can be an important stimulus for local governments to actively improve their capacity. Regular meetings and citizen councils can increase the pressure on local leaders to turn popular demands into outputs. Local government responsiveness, one of the main rationales for decentralizing, cannot be improved when there are no mechanisms for transferring information between the local government and its constituents. Decentralization is seen as a means of improving the planning and implementation of national development especially those concerned with rural development, and facilitating effective popular participation in the process of development in a more profound way which is sought partly as a means of making plans more relevant to local needs and enlisting local support in their implementation, thereby also helping to improve the quality of rural development efforts. The Lack of such community participation if not prevent decentralization from achieving its goals; it does limit its ability to create large efficiency gains.

In order to enhance the participation of the community at different levels the capacity building program has included grassroots participation as one of the sub-programs of DLDP that aimed at enhancing democratic participation and empowerment of the rural woreda population at the grassroots level in affairs affecting their lives in the development and democratic process. Accordingly, in order to measure the level of participation of the community, respondents were asked to rate the participation of the community in local development and 43 (39.8%) of Gindeberet woreda and 26 (41.3%) of Abuna Gindeberet woreda respondents indicated the availability of adequate level of community participation while 33 (30.6%) of the former woreda and 24 (38.1%) of the later woreda exposed the low and high degree of community participation respectively.

Decentralization is perceived as bringing government closer to the people, leading to greater political participation at the local level, with citizens more able to make claims on local government and to subject it to greater scrutiny. In turn, it is predicted that local government will be more knowledgeable about and more responsive to the needs of local population. Accordingly, in order to address whether local administration makes regular meetings with the community 71 (65.7%) of Gindeberet woreda and 30 (47.6%) of Abuna Gindeberet woreda respondents exhibited that the local government administration is short of having regular meetings with the constituents while 30 (27.8%) of the former woreda and 23 (36.5%) of the later woreda concluded that the local government administration's meetings with the community is at acceptable level. Besides, 7 (6.5%) of Gindeberet woreda and 10 (15.9%) of Abuna Gindeberet woreda respondents specified the availability of high level of local government administration meetings with the community.

Decentralizing responsibility for managing local affairs and for local development at the local level rather than central government will afford citizens greater access to, and ability to influence, the policy/ decision-making process. Accordingly, to assess the level of participation of the people in the planning and implementation of local development the survey result revealed the presence of reasonable degree of community participation in development policy planning and implementation as 53(49.1%) of Gindeberet woreda and 29(46%) of Abuna Gindeberet woreda respondents ranked satisfactory. Furthermore, 39 (36.1%) of Gindeberet woreda and 19 (30.2%) of Abuna Gindeberet woreda respondents indicated the low degree of participation of the community while the remaining 16 (14.8%) of the former woreda and 15 (23.8%) of the later woreda exhibited the high degree of participation of the community in planning and implementation of local development policies. Even though there is significant changes and improvement in terms of community participation, the focus group discussion also come to reach the consensus that community participation is not to the desired level due to lack of awareness on the part of the public, and the limited efforts of local government leaders to convince the public. However, the people are represented by district council that plans and evaluate the development process in the locality.

Theoretically, local governments have the autonomy to set priorities and targets about their localities. In this regard, an assessment was made whether local development activities have given priorities to community interest, and 68 (63%) of Gindeberet woreda and 32 (50.8%) of Abuna Gindeberet woreda respondents indicated as low and satisfactory respectively whereas 37 (34.3%) of former woreda and 23 (36.5%) of Abuna Gindeberet woreda rated as satisfactory and low respectively. Moreover, the remaining 3 (2.8%) of Gindeberet woreda and 8 (12.7%) of Abuna Gindeberet woreda regarded whether local development activities have given priorities of the community as high. The Abuna Gindeberet woreda is better off in terms of addressing the priorities of the community than Gindeberet woreda.

In light of this respondents were asked the degree to which the local government administration is addressing the socio-economic problems of the local community, and 80 (74.1%) of Gindeberet woreda and 30 (47.6%) of Abuna Gindeberet woreda respondents clarified the low level of local government effort to address the socio-economic problems of the local community while 24 (22.2%) of former woreda and 22 (34.9%) of the later woreda rated the same issue as satisfactory. Moreover, 4 (3.7%) of Gindeberet woreda and 11 (17.5%) of Abuna Gindeberet woreda respondents demonstrated the effort made by local government administration as high. The Focus group discussion also revealed the presence of efforts to make the socio-economic problems of the woreda the concern of woreda sector offices however; there are still limitations to this issue that emanated from lack of planning experts, lack of adequate human resources, and lack of capacity of offices.

Planning for local development is achieved through a participatory process in which the partners set a collective vision for local development, agree on common goals, and on strategies/ plans for achieving the goals and realizing the vision, and development plans produced through such a process will enjoy full support/commitment of the local community, and therefore is very likely to be realized, unlike the usual fate of centrally produced plans. With regards to whether plans of the offices are communicated to the stakeholders 68 (63%) of Gindeberet woreda and 33 (52.4%) of Abuna Gindeberet woreda respondents revealed that the plans of offices are not made to be known by different stakeholders while 35(32.4%) of former woreda and 25 (39.7%) of the later woreda respondents showed the acceptable degree to which local level stakeholders are informed about the plans of the offices. Furthermore, 5 (4.6%) of Gindeberet woreda and 5 (7.9%) of

Abuna Gindeberet woreda respondents uncovered the extent to which local stakeholders are made to know the plans of the office as high.

Decentralization brings government closer to the people, and thus enables citizens to be better informed and to better understand the conduct of public business. This facilitates the forging of a strong relationship and coordination between the governors and the governed as well as enhances the accountability of public officials to their constituents. With regards to the coordination and communication between the community and woreda level offices, 73 (67.6%) of Gindeberet woreda and 33 (52.4%) of Abuna Gindeberet woreda respondents specified the low level of the coordination and communication between the community and woreda offices whereas 31 (28.7%) of former wereda and 22 (34.9%) of Abuna Gindeberet woreda respondents regarded the same issue as satisfactory. Moreover, the remaining 4 (3.7%) of Gindeberet woreda and 8 (12.7%) of Abuna Gindeberet woreda respondents ranked the same issue as high.

Non-governmental organizations can often be a source of trained, experienced personnel, and sources of finance. In assessing the community's longer term capacity, the depth and history of civil society organizations should be considered. Accordingly, the history of civil society in both localities is a recent phenomenon as there are only single NGOs in the woredas under study that was established in 2010. With regards to the linkages between local government and NGOs 50 (46.3%) of Gindeberet woreda and 32 (50.8%) of Abuna Gindeberet woreda respondents rated the issue as satisfactory and low respectively whereas 44 (40.7%) of former woreda and 21 (33.3%) of the later wereda rated the same issue as low and satisfactory respectively. Moreover, the remaining 14 (13%) of Gindeberet woreda and 10 (15.9%) of Abuna Gindeberet woreda respondents rated as high. In connection with this, respondents were asked whether NGOs and donors consult woredas while planning and 67 (62%) of Gindeberet woreda and 30 (47.6%) of Abuna Gindeberet woreda respondents rated as low while 32 (29.6%) of former woreda and 23 (36.5%) of the later wereda rated it as acceptable. Further, the remaining 9 (8.3%) of Gindeberet woreda and 10 (15.9%) of Abuna Gindeberet woreda respondents evaluated the same issue as high. Similarly, respondents were asked whether woredas consult NGOs and donors while planning and 80 (74.1%) of Gindeberet woreda and 40 (63.5%) of Abuna Gindeberet woreda respondents regarded it as low whereas 25 (23.1%) of the former woreda and 18 (28.6%) of later woreda respondents rated it as satisfactory. Furthermore, 3 (2.8%) of Gindeberet woreda and 5 (7.9%) of Abuna Gindeberet woreda respondents rated similar issue as high.

Besides, respondents were asked the level of linkages between the local government and CBOs and 69 (63.9%) of Gindeberet woreda and 30 (47.6%) of Abuna Gindeberet woreda respondents revealed that the low degree of interaction between local government and CBOs whereas 36 (33.3%) of the former woreda and 28 (44.4%) of Abuna Gindeberet woreda respondents regarded the interaction between the two as satisfactory. Moreover, the remaining 3 (2.8%) of Gindeberet woreda and 5 (7.9%) of Abuna Gindeberet woreda rated the same issue as high.

Furthermore, the capacity of the community is not only measured by the history of civil societies in the local governments but it also need to take into account the history of private organization, their roles to be the source of trained, competent and skilled human resources as well as viable sources of finance and other resources as well as their interaction with the local government. Accordingly, the focus group discussion revealed the absence of strong and dependable private organizations that have coordination and communication with local governance actors. Hence, it is possible to deduce that local governance actors in the study area do not recognize the presence of each other as the linkages between NGOs and the local government on the one hand and between that of the private organization and NGOs as well as ones more the interaction between private organization and local government is weak and fragile.

Chapter Four

4. Conclusions and Recommendations

4.1. Conclusions

Decentralization involves the shift of planning, managing, implementing and evaluation authority and responsibility from higher tiers of government to possible lower tiers of government. It is about transferring power and authority to several different actors and agencies that include private organizations, public institutions, corporations as well as civil service organizations.

Irrespective of its uncertain success rate, different government, development planners, donor institutions have continued to promote decentralization on the basis of different justifications, viz. it is a tool to bring about political stability and control ethnic uprisings, promote accountability, increase community participation at different levels, ensure allocative efficiency, and achieve equity and distributional goals more. Devolved form of governance is taken as the most effective, efficient and responsive form of decentralization since it confers authority and responsibility in resource mobilization and investment decisions and increases popular participation that creates or opens more political space to pertinent actors.

In light of the above theoretical justification Ethiopia has adapted decentralization as an excellent medication to its problems that were seen under the previous centralized systems of governance. To this end, decentralization was undertaken in two phases with decentralization at regional level followed by woreda decentralization that empowered woredas to deliver public services under the mandate of regional and zonal level of governments. However, different studies indicated that woredas could not discharge their functions and responsibilities due to lack of financial and human resources, lack of proper legal and administrative rules, regulations, directives and guidelines, lack of autonomy, etc.

In order to alleviate these problems and challenges at rural woreda the government has initiated District Level Decentralization Program (DLDP) as one component of capacity building programs in 2001. Accordingly, the Oromia National Regional State have provided woredas under its revised constitution of 2001 the power to prepare and approve their own budget, prepare and implement economic and social development projects, set up and manage public services and exercise democratic decision making at the local level. Gindeberet and Abuna Gindeberet Woreda being one of the woredas in Oromia National Regional States were part and part of the reform programs.

The capacity building initiative at local level was launched with an intention to improve the performance of decentralized units as capacity building at all government levels is considered as an essential component of decentralization. In light of this, this study was conducted with the purpose to assess the capacity of woredas since the implementation of District Level Decentralization Program.

Accordingly, the study was conducted with an intention to achieve the following specific objectives, viz. to assess the human resource development (training and development), to assess human resource capacities, assess the availability of the necessary materials or logistics necessary to the successful implementations of local development plans and functions, to identify the financial capacity of the woredas under study, assess the existing enabling environments (both internal and external enabling environments), and to assess the extent of community participation in local development planning, monitoring and implementations.

However, the study showed that the implementation of District Level Decentralization Program has brought about insignificant changes to the existing woreda situations under study. This negligible outcome of capacity building programs could be discovered in light of the above mentioned objectives.

Even though woredas were given the autonomy to plan, administer and manage public services and other issues that falls within their jurisdictions, practically woreda autonomy has not been fully operationalized particularly of personnel administration. In this regard, regional government and zonal administration intervention to personnel administration like in the issue of hiring, firing, promotions, transfers, etc. are identified as some of the impediments to woreda autonomy. Furthermore, woredas have limited autonomy to set priorities and targets and decide on the budget allocated to them. Local governments are compelled to set their priorities and targets in light of national and regional government's priorities by setting aside the priority of their locality and constituencies. Besides, the proportion of recurrent and capital budget is decided by the regional government.

The woreda planning and budgeting process is not participatory as plans and budget are approved only by members of cabinets and woreda councils without the inclusion of the opinions of experts. This have resulted in deteriorated service delivery and decreased the commitment and interest of staffs to the plan.
Because of lack of budget, ever expanding of sectoral offices, and merging and abolition of offices, woredas have lack of adequate and qualified human resources to discharge their decentralized duties and responsibilities. Besides, even those filled positions are not properly occupied as most employees are assigned arbitrary without their profession and areas of specializations. Moreover, the study indicated that the performance of managers in the study area were unlikely as they held positions based on political loyalty than professionalism, and lack of on job training to improve their performance.

Due to lack of budget and qualified manpower to deliver the training, training programs are not adequate. Trainings are short term, centralized, and mostly provided to top level woreda officials and core process owners. Trainings are not provided based on need assessment that makes them supply driven than demand led. In addition, human resource development not only involves training but also various incentives. However, there were no incentives provided for employees in woredas because of lack of budget; and no standard benchmarks upon which the performance of employee was to be rated. These have decreased employee commitment and creativity that leads to high rate of employee turnover and deteriorated the effective implementation of plans.

Woredas have lack of financial capacity to finance their decentralized mandates due to the presence of limited sources of revenue and capacity to generate revenue that forced them to rely for more than 80% of their annual budget on grants from the regional government. These was traced to lack of human resources, lack of skilled and competent managers and staffs, tax evasion, lack of sufficient budget, lack of awareness on the side of tax payers, topographic influence and the expansion of illegal business as well as woreda revenue authority's load with extra works.

Moreover, little attention has been given to the development of infrastructures and office facilities in Gindeberet and Abuna Gindeberet woredas as basic office equipment such as telephone, vehicles, internet service, computer net workings and offices among others are hardly available that affected the coordination and communication among decentralized units and sectoral offices.

The internal enabling environment of Woredas is highly weak and fragile. This can be demonstrated through lack of appropriate, clear, simple, and stable work structure, lack of incentives and regular meetings with staffs, lack of monitoring and evaluation capacity of local governments. Further, lack of rules, directives, procedures, laws, and guidelines as well as lack of appropriate job descriptions was also noticed that highly complicated the coordination and integration of decentralized activities as well as inhibited the ability of implementing agency staffs to interact with higher level authorities.

The limited presence of communication of directives, rules, laws, guidelines regarding the duties and powers of woredas, lack of local level actors awareness of the vision of decentralization, the inadequacy of coordination and communication among or between different levels of governments and actors, and the weak support from the regional government *inter alia* have made the overall enabling external environment of local government not conducive to work. Moreover, capacity building was implemented with an intention to bring about substantial improvement to the effort of decentralization at local level nevertheless; this objective was not materialized as intended.

Community participation is considered as an essential component of decentralization as decentralized decision making enlarges opportunities for improved planning and implementation of national development goals especially those concerned with rural development. Accordingly, in order to enhance the participation of the community at grassroots level, participation was included as one of the concerns of DLDP that aimed at enhancing democratic participation and empowerment of the rural woreda population in affairs affecting their life in development and democratic process.

Though the participation of the community in matters of planning and implementation of local development is improved, due to lack of awareness on the part of the community about the benefits of participation and the limited effort of local leaders to convince the public, the participation of the community in most issues affecting their life is not to the desired level. Above all local government's limited attention to the priority and interest, and the socio-economic problems of the local community as well as the existence of weak coordination and communication between different governance actors were factors that limited popular participation.

Moreover, the history of NGOs in the study area is a recent phenomenon. The scope of the participation of NGOs in addressing local priority is also found to be limited. The interaction and coordination between NGOs and the local government is weak. Further, there were no strong private enterprises that actively participate in local development.

4.2 Recommendations

Depending on the conclusions drawn the following possible recommendations are forwarded:

- In order to motivate and stimulate employees to be committed, creative and productive the incentive system and the human resource development in the study areas is weak. Therefore, to address this both monetary (like salary) and non-monetary rewards (such as promotion, and other types of rewards) should come in to force. To this end, the initiatives should be reinforced through the preparation of clear rules, directives, laws, procedures and regulations. Furthermore, the training programs offered are inadequate, not demand driven, as well as woredas lack budget allocated to training programs. Hence, training has to be improved both in quality and quantity through allocation of adequate budget, and assigning qualified and skilled trainers to the proper position.

- Even though the regional constitution clearly stipulates the autonomy of woredas in matters of planning and execution of matters that falls within their jurisdiction, practically woredas are under strict supervision and control of the Zonal administration and the regional government. This is manifested through the limited autonomy woredas have on human resource management and financial matters. Hence, rather than trespassing the autonomy of woredas, it is proper to reinforce their efforts through directives, guidelines, proclamations, etc. so that woredas could use it as a bench mark. Moreover, the regional government needs to capacitate employees who held the position of human resource management through different trainings. The local governments under study have to allocate sufficient budgets to fill the vacant positions this effort also needs to be reinforced by regional government.

- Woredas lack the necessary capacity to generate adequate revenue that compelled them to heavily rely on grants they obtain from the regional government. Furthermore, they lack autonomy to decide on the grant. Hence, in order to overcome such financial constraints, the tax collection system needs to be modernized; the capacity of woredas needs to be improved through training, hiring qualified and adequate human resources and allocating adequate budget. Moreover, there have to be inter-organizational linkages and communication to control illegal business. Besides, different offices and stakeholders have to work toward raising the awareness of the community about the benefits of tax and revenue.

- In order to ensure the proper utilizations of resources, the regional government should consider the current work structure that do not allow the presence of internal auditor and fill vacant positions with adequate and qualified staffs.

- Infrastructures and office equipment are critical inputs to discharge the mandates and responsibilities of any level of government. However, Woredas have lack of facilities necessary to carry out their day to day activities. Thus, to ensure access to facilities the government has to create linkages with donors and NGOs as well as with private organizations and individuals so that they may sponsor them. Moreover, regional government has to allocate extra funds to finance the facility needs of Woredas as local governments' lacks adequate resources.

- Woredas lacks conducive work environment. Hence, in order to improve the working environment every layer of government needs to keep the structure of the organization stable, simple and clear, and sound policies, favorable incentives, effective coordination and communication need to be created among or between different sectoral offices and layers of government. Furthermore, the presence of laws, policies, directives, procedures, and guidelines should be considered.

- In order to enhance the participation of the community local leaders has to work towards convincing and make aware the community about the benefits of participation. Furthermore, the local government needs to get the trust of the people through addressing the socio-economic and the priority of the society. Besides, regular meetings and discussions needs to be conducted. In order to attract other local governance actors (civil society and private actors) the local government has to arrange different incentives. Furthermore, the linkage among these actors has to be strengthened.

References

African Capacity Building Foundation (ACBF) (2011). **Africa Capacity Indicators 2011: Capacity Development in Fragile States.** South Africa: Ultra Litho (PTY) Ltd.

Antwi-Boasiako, K. Badu (2010). **'Public administration: Local Government and Decentralization in Ghana.'** Journal of African Studies and Development Vol. 2(7), pp. 166-175.

Asmelash Beyene (2000). "Decentralization as a tool for Resolving the Nationality Problem: the Ethiopian Experience". Regional Development Dialogue 21(2): 122–147. Retrieved from http:www.4shared.com/document/jUnz-kiQ/A_Nation_in_perpetual_Transiti.html

Assefa Fiseha (2006). "Theory versus Practice in the Implementation of Ethiopia's Ethnic Federalism." In David Turton, (ed.), **Ethnic Federalism: the Ethiopian Experience in Comparative Perspective,** pp. 131–164. Oxford: James Carrey.

Babbie, Earl (1973). **Survey Research Methods.** Belmont, California: Wadsworth Pub.

Babbie, Earl (1986). **The Practice of Social Research(** 4th ed.). Belmont, California: Wadsworth Publishing Co.

Baser, Heather, and Morgan Peter (2008). '**Capacity, Change and Performance.** 'European Center for Development Policy Management. Study Report. http://siteresources. Worldbank .org/INTCDRC/Resources/CapacityChangePerformanceReport.pdf

Brinkerhoff, Derick W. (2010). '**Developing Capacity in Fragile States.** 'Public Administration and Development Vol. 30, Pp.66–78.

Browne, Stephen (2002). **Introduction: Rethinking capacity development. Retrieved from** http://unpan1 .un.org/intradoc/groups/public/documents/un/unpan005787.pdf

Cheema, G. Shabbir and Rondinelli, Dennis A. (2007).'From Government Decentralization to Decentralized Governance.' In Cheema, G. Shabbir and Rondinelli, Dennis A. (eds.), **Decentralizing Governance: Emerging Concepts and Practices.** Washington, D.C.: Brookings Institution Press. Pp. 1-23

Civil Society Human and Institutional Development Programme (CHIP) (2007). **Capacity building Framework for Partners and Stakeholders.** Retrieved from http://foreverindus. org/pdf/ capacity-building_framework.pdf

Conyers, Diana (2006). **'Decentralization: The Latest Fashion in Development Administration?.'** Research in Public Policy Analysis and Management, Volume 15, 447–462.

Crawford, Gordon and Hartmann, Christof (2008). 'Introduction: Decentralization as a Pathway out of Poverty and Conflict?.' In Crawford, Gordon and Hartmann, Christof (eds.), **Decentralization in Africa: A Pathway out of Poverty and Conflict?.** Amsterdam: Amsterdam University Press. Pp. 1-32.

Creswell, John W. (2009). **Research Design: Qualitative, Quantitative and Mixed Methods Approaches.** (3rd ed.). London: SAGE Publications Ltd.

Daniel Gamachu (1994). **A Nation in Perpetual Transition: The Politics of Changes in Administrative Divisions and Subdivisions in Ethiopia.** Papers of the 12th International Conference Ethiopian Studies. Addis Ababa University.

Dawson, Catherine (2007). **A practice Guide to Research Methods: A user Friendly Manual for Mastering Research Techniques and Projects** (3rd ed.). United Kingdom: Spring Hill House.

Devas, Nick (2006). 'The Challenges of Decentralization.' In Alam, Munawwar and Nickson, Andrew (eds.), **Managing Change in Local Governance.** Managing the Public Service Strategies for Improvement Series No. 15. United Kingdom: Marlborough House. Pp. 33-50.

Dickovick, J. Tyler and Tegegne Gebre-Egziabher (2010). **Comparative Assessment of Decentralization in Africa**: Ethiopia Desk Study. http://www.usaid. Gov/ our_work/democracy _and_governance/publications/pdfs/ethiopia_desk_study.pdf

Eade, Deborah (2003). 'Preface.' In Eade, Deborah (ed.), Development Methods and Approaches Critical Reflections. UK: Oxfam GB.

Faguet, Jean-Paul (1997). **'Technical Consultation on Decentralization: Decentralization and Local Government Performance.'** FAO, Rome, December 16-18, 1997.

Farrell, Cynthia (2007). **The CHF Capacity Building Approach.Ottawa: CHF.**

Federal Democratic Republic of Ethiopia. (1995). **Federal Constitution, Addis Ababa**

Federal Democratic Republic of Ethiopia. (2007). **Emerging Regions Development Program (ERDP).** Ministry of Federal Affairs, Addis Ababa.

Fenta Mandefro (1998). 'Decentralization Policies and Implementations: The Case of Ethiopia. In Alemayehu Molla and Tsegabrhan Mekonen (eds.), **Managerial Capacity Development in Ethiopia.** Proceeding of the Third Annual Conference on Management in Ethiopia. Addis Ababa: EMPA. Pp. 189-213.

Flick, Uwe (2002). **An Introduction to Qualitative Research** (2nd ed.). London: SAGE Publications Ltd.

Fowler, Alan and Ubels, Jan (2010). 'The Multi-faceted Nature of Capacity: Two Leading Frameworks'. In Ubels, Jan et.al., (eds.), **Capacity Development in Practice.** London and Washington, D. C.: Earthscan. Pp. 11-24.

Fukuda-Parr, Sakiko (2002). 'Overview: Institutional innovations for capacity development.' In Fukuda-Parr, Sakiko et.al., (eds.), **Capacity for Development: New Solutions to Old Problems.** UK and USA: Earthscan Publications Ltd. Pp. 1-22.

Gay, L. (1981). **Educational Research Competencies for Analysis and Application (** 2nd ed.). New York: Charles E Merrill.

Gbla, Osman and Rugumamu, Severine (2003). **Studies in Reconstruction and Capacity Building in Post-Conflict Countries in Africa: Some Lessons of Experience from Mozambique.** South Africa: African Capacity Building Foundation.

Hadingham, Tim (2003). **'Decentralization and Development Planning: Some Practical Considerations.'** Retrieved from

http://www.ilo.org/wcmsp5/groups/public/@ed_emp/@emp_policy/@invest/documents/publication/wcms_asist_8213.pdf

Horton, Douglas (2002). **'Planning, Implementing, and Evaluating Capacity Development.'** Briefing Paper No.50, International Service for National Agricultural Research, July 2002.

Joint UNDP-Government of Germany Evaluation of the UNDP Role in Decentralization and Local Governance (1999). **'Decentralization: A Sampling of Definitions.'** Working Paper Prepared in Connection with the Joint UNDP-Government of Germany Evaluation of the UNDP Role in Decentralization and local Governance.

Kaplan, Allan (2000). '**Capacity Building: Shifting the Paradigms of Practice.'** Development in Practice, Vol. 10, No.3 & 4. UK: Oxfam GB. Pp. 517-526.

Katorobo, James (2005). **'Decentralization and Local Autonomy for Participatory Democracy.'**6th Global Forum on Reinventing Government Towards Participatory and Transparent Governance 24 – 27 May 2005, Seoul, Republic of Korea.

Koning, Jaap De et.al. (2006). '**Evaluation of the ESF Support to Capacity Building.'** Final Report. Retrieved from http://www.seor.nl/media/publications/evaluation-esf-support-capacity-building.pdf

Kothari, C.R. (2004). **Research Methodology: Methods and Techniques.** (2nd ed.). New Delhi: New Age International (P) Ltd.

Kumar, Ranjit (1999). **Research Methodology: A step-by-Step Guide for Beginners.** London: SAGE Publications Ltd.

Lavergne, Réal, and Saxby, John (2001). **'Capacity Development: Vision and Implications.'** Canada: Canadian International Development Agency Occasional Series No. 3.

Léautier, Frannie et.al., (2010). **Capacity Building and Skills Development as Prime Mechanisms for Africa's Socio-Economic Transformation: Lessons from ACBF's Interventions.** ACBF Working Paper No. 16.

Lister, Stephen, and Betley, Mary (1999). **'Approaches to Decentralisation in developing countries.'** Paper Prepared as Background Reading for the MEFMI/DFID Workshop on Good Practicein Public Expenditure Management, Cape town June 1999.

Litvack, Jennie et.al., (1998). **'Rethinking Decentralization in Developing Countries.'** Washington, D.C.: World Bank.

Lopes, Carlos, and Thomas Theison (2003). **Ownership, Leadership and Transformation: Can We Do Better for Capacity Development?.** London: Earthscan Publications Ltd.

Lusthaus, Charles et.al., (1995). **Institutional Assessment: A Framework for Strengthening Organizational Capacity for IDRC's Research Partners.** Ottawa: International Development Research Centre.

Lusthaus, Charles, et.al., (1999).**'Capacity Development: Definitions, Issues and Implications for Planning, Monitoring and Evaluation.'**Universalia Occasional Paper No. 35.

Lusthaus, Charles et.al.,(2002). **Organizational Assessment: A Framework for Improving Performance.** Ottawa, Washington, D.C.: International Development Research Centre and Inter-American Development Bank.

Mackay, Ronald et.al., (2002). 'Evaluating Organizational Capacity Development.' **The Canadian Journal of Program Evaluation** Vol. 17 No. 2 Pp. 121–150.

Malik,Khalid (2002). 'Capacity and Development: Towards a normative framework: Technical cooperation, capacities and development.' In Fukuda-Parr, Sakiko et.al., (eds.), **Capacity for Development: New Solutions to Old Problems.** UK and USA: Earthscan Publications Ltd. Pp. 23-42.

Meheret Ayenew (2002). 'Decentralization in Ethiopia: Two Case Studies on Devolution of Power and Responsibilities to Local Government Authorities.' In Bahru Zewde and Siegfried Pausewang (eds.) **Ethiopia: The Challenge of Democracy from Below.** Nordiska Afrikainstitutet, Uppsala and Forum for social Studies, Addis Ababa. Pp. 130-146.

Middleton, John et.al., (1987). **'Designing Management for Uncertainly and Innovationin Education Project.'** Discussion Paper Education and Training Series, Report No. EDT75. Washigton, D.C.: World Bank.

Miller, Keithl (2002). **'Advantages & Disadvantages of Local Government Decentralization: A Presentation to the Caribbean Conference on Local Government & Decentralization.'** Georgetown, Guyana: June 25-28, 2002.

Ministry of Finance and Economic Development (MOFED) (2002). **Ethiopia: Sustainable Development and Poverty Reduction Program.** Ethiopia, Addis Ababa: MOFED.

Neuman, Larence W. (1994). **Social Research Methods: Qualitative and Quantitative Approaches** (2nd ed.). Bosto: Allyn and Bacon.

Olowu, Dele (2001). **'Decentralization Policies and Practices under Structural Adjustment and Democratization in Africa.'** Democracy, Governance and Human Rights Program Paper No.4, Geneva: United Nations Research Institute for Social Development.

Olowu, Dele, and Wunsch,James S. (2004). **Local Governance in Africa: The Challenges of Democratic Decentralization.** Boulder and London: Lynne Rienner.

Organization for Economic Co-operation and Development (OECD) (2006). **The Challenge of Capacity Development: Working Towards Good Practice.** Paris: OECD.

Oromia National Regional State (2008).Oromia National Regional State Revised Cnstitution (3rd ed.). No.46/2001,Magalata Oromia, Finfinne.

Parker, Andrew N., and Kirsten, Johann (1995). **'Decentralization: Toward A Revitalized Strategy for Rural Development.'**Agrekon. Vol. 34, No. 4, Pp. 242-249.

Pausewang, Siegfried (1994). 'Local Democracy and Central Control.' In Abebe Zegeye and Siegfried Pausewang (eds.), **Ethiopia in Change: Peasantry, Nationalism and Democracy.** London: British Academia Press.

Peace Building Commission Working Group on Lessons Learned (WGLL) (2007). **'Background Note: Local Governance and Decentralization in Postwar Contexts.'** Retrieved from http://www.un.org/fr/peacebuilding/wgll/decentralization_governance/wgll_background_note_13_12_07.pdf

Peltenburg, Monique (1996). **Building Capacity for Better Cities.** Rotterdam: Institute for Housing and Urban Development Studies.

Punch, Keith F. (1998) **Introduction to Social Research: Quantitative and Qualitative Approaches.** London: SAGE Publications Ltd.

Raj Panday, Devendra (2002). 'Technical Cooperation and Institutional Capacity-Building for Development: Back to the Basics.' In Fukuda-Parr, Sakiko et.al., (eds.), **Capacity for Development: New Solutions to Old Problems.** UK and USA: Earthscan Publications Ltd. Pp. 61-84.

Rondinelli, Dennis A. (1999). 'What and Why.' In Litvack, Jennie and Seddon, Jessica (eds.), **Decentralization Briefing Notes.** Washington, D.C.: World Bank. Pp. 1-8.

Rondinelli, Dennis A. et.al., (1983) **'Decentralization in Developing Countries: A Review of Recent Experience.'** World Bank Staff Working Papers No.581, Management and Development Series No.8. Washington, D.C.: The International Bank for Reconstruction and Development / World Bank.

Rondinelli, Dennis A. et.al., (1989). **'Analyzing Decentralization Policies in Developing Countries: a Political-Economy Framework.'** Development and Change (SAGE, London, Newbury Park and New Delhi), Vol. 20, 57-87.

Seddon,Jessica and Tommas D., Gtulio (1999). 'Civil Service Reform and Decentralization' in in Litvack, Jennie and Seddon, Jessica (eds.), **Decentralization Briefing Notes.** Washington, D.C.: World Bank. Pp. 39-42.

Shah, Anwar, and Thompson, Theresa (2004). **'Implementing Decentralized Local Governance: A Treacherous Road with Potholes, Detours and Road Closures.'** World Bank Policy Research Working Paper 3353, Washington, D.C.: World Bank.

Smillie, Ian (2001). 'From Patrons to Partners?' In Smillie, Ian (ed.). **Patronage or Partnership: Local Capacity Building in Humanitarian Crises.** United States of America: Kumarian Press, Inc. Pp. 175-194.

Smillie, Ian (2001). 'Capacity Building and the Humanitarian Enterprise.' In Smillie, Ian (ed.), **Patronage or Partnership: Local Capacity Building in Humanitarian Crises.** United States of America: Kumarian Press, Inc. Pp. 7-23.

Smoke, Paul (2003). **'Decentralization in Africa: Goals, Dimensions, Myths and Challenges.'** New York: John Wiley & Sons, Ltd. Public Administration and Development 23, 7–16.

Smoke, Paul (2001). **'Fiscal Decentralization in Developing Countries: A Review of Current Concepts and Practice.'** Democracy, Governance and Human Rights Program Paper No. 2, Geneva: United Nations Research Institute for Social Development.

Sustainable Development and Poverty Reduction Program (2002)

Tegegne Gebre-Egziabher (2007). **Introduction:** A Brief Overview of Decentralization in Ethiopia. Retrieved from www.africanbookscollective.com/.../decentralization-in-ethiopia/

Tegegne Gebre-Egziabher and Kassahun Birhanu (2004). **"The Role of Decentralized Governance in Building Local Institutions, Diffusing Ethnic Conflicts and Alleviating Poverty in Ethiopia".** Regional Development Dialogue 25(1): 35–63.

Turay, T. Mark (2001). 'Sierra Leone: Peace Building in Purgatory.' In Smillie, Ian (ed.), **Patronage or Partnership: Local Capacity Building in Humanitarian Crises.** United States of America: Kumarian Press, Inc. Pp. 157-174.

Ubels, Jan et.al., (2010). 'A Resource Volume on Capacity Development.' In Ubels, Jan et.al., (eds.) **Capacity Development in Practice.** London and Washington, D. C.: Earthscan. Pp. 1-8.

UNCRD (1996). **Local Governance and Local Economic Development: Capacity Building Case Studies in Asia and Latin America.** Nagowa: UNCRD

UN-HABITAT (2002). Local **Democracy and Decentralization in East and Southern: Experiences from Uganda, Kenya, Botswana, Tanzania and Ethiopia.** Global Campaign on Urban Governance. Retrieved from http://www.unhabitat.org/pmss/ getElectronicVersion.asp? nr=1148&alt=1

United Nations (2006).**'Definition of Basic Concepts and Terminologies in Governance and Public Administration.'** Committee of Experts on Public Administration, Fifth session, New York, 27-31 March 2006.

United Nations Development Program (UNDP) (1997). **Capacity Development.** Technical Advisory Paper 2. New York: United Nations Development Program Management Development and Governance Division Bureau for Policy Development.

United Nations Development Program (UNDP) (2009). **Supporting Capacity Development: The UNDP Approach.** New York: UNDP.

UNDP/UNCDF. (2005). **Local Development Project: North Gonder Zone, Amhara National Regional State.** Project Document.

Van der Loop, Theo (ed.). (2002). **Local Democracy and Decentralization in Ethiopia.** Regional and Local Development Studies, Addis Ababa University.

Walters, Hettie (2007) **'Capacity Development, Institutional Change and Theory of Change: What do we mean and where are the linkages.'** A Conceptual Background Paper.http://portals.wi.wur.nl/files/docs/successfailuredevelopment/Walters_CapacityDevelopmentConceptPaperFIN.pdf

Woodhill, Jim (2010). 'Capacity Lives Between Multiple Stakeholders.' In Ubels, Jan et.al., (eds.), **Capacity Development in Practice.** London and Washington, D. C.: Earthscan. Pp. 25-41.

Worku Yehualeshet (2005). 'District Decentralization in Ethiopia: Expenditure Assignment and Fiscal Transfer.' In Tegegne GebrEgziabher and Meine Peter VanDijk (eds.), **Issues and Challenges in Local and Regional Development.** Addis Ababa: United Printers. Pp. 29-58.

World Bank (2005). **Building Effective States: Forging Engaged Societies.** Washington, D.C.: World Bank Task Force on Capacity Development in Africa.

World Bank (2005). **Capacity Building in Africa: An OED Evaluation of World Bank Support.** Washington, D.C.: World Bank

World Bank (1996). **Local Government Capacity in Colombia: Beyond Technical Assistance.** Washington D.C.: World Bank.

Wunsch, James S. (2001). **'Decentralization, Local Governance and 'Recentralization in Africa.'** New York: John Wiley & Sons, Ltd. Public Administration and Development 21, 277-288.

Wunsch, James S. (2008). **'Why has Decentralization Failed in Africa? Assessing the Lessons of Self- organized, Local Governance Initiatives.'**http://www.indiana.edu/~workshop/ seminars/papers/wunsch_mcpaper08.pdf

Yigremew Adal (2001). **'Decentralization and Local Governance in Post Dergue Ethiopia.'** In Berhanu Mengistu and Elizabeth Vogel, MHSA (eds.), Governance and Sustainable Development: Promoting Collaborative Partnerships. pp.103-111. Addis Ababa, Ethiopia.

Yigremew Adal, et.al. (2005). **Study on the Implementation of Decentralization Policy in Ethiopia.** AddisAbaba: Oxfam GB Ethiopia Publications.

Zemelak Ayele (2009), **Decentralization and Local Governance in Ethiopia. Local Government Bulletin Conference,23 July 2009**. Retrieved from http://www.communitylawcentre. org.za/clc-projects/local-government/10th-anniversary-of-the-local-government-bulletin/Zemelak%20Ayele.pdf

Unpublished Documents

Abuna Gindeberet Wereda Budget Proclamation of 2002 Fiscal Year

Abuna Gindeberet Wereda Budget Proclamation of 2003 Fiscal Year

Abuna Gindeberet Wereda Budget Proclamation of 2004 Fiscal Year

Abuna Gindeberet Wereda Second round Budget Proclamation of 2003 Fiscal Year

Abuna Gindeberet Wereda Second round Budget Proclamation of 2004 Fiscal Year

Gindeberet Wereda Budget Proclamation of 2002 Fiscal Year

Gindeberet Wereda Budget Proclamation of 2003 Fiscal Year

Gindeberet Wereda Budget Proclamation of 2004 Fiscal Year

Gindeberet Wereda Second round Budget Proclamation of 2002 Fiscal Year

Gindeberet Wereda Second round Budget Proclamation of 2003 Fiscal Year

Gindeberet Wereda Second round Budget Proclamation of 2004 Fiscal Year

Documents Indicating Human Resources of Gindeberet Weredas Sectoral offices

Oromia National Regional State Local Governments Block Grant Allocation Formula

Focus Group Discussion

Date: 14/04/2012 Time 02:15-05:33AM in Gindeberet Wereda at TVET premise

Date: 19/04/2012 Time 08:56-11:15PM in Abuna Gindeberet Wereda Office of Finance and Economic Development.

Annex-1

Addis Ababa University, School of Graduate Studies
Public Administration and Development Management

Capacity Building for Decentralized Local Governance: The case of Gindebebret and Abuna Gindeberet Woreda in Oromia National Regional State

Dear Respondents,

The aim of the research is to collect valuable information about the capacity of local governments, and capacity building efforts to the decentralization process and local governance in Gindeberet and Abuna Gindeberet Wereda under the title ***'Capacity Building for Decentralized Local Governance: The Case of Gindeberet and Abuna Gindeberet Woredas in Oromia National Regional State.'*** The data gathered from you will only be used for academic purpose, for M.A. thesis in Public Management and Policy, not for any other purpose. Therefore your definite data and answers are highly appreciated and will be kept confidential.

Thank you for your cooperation

Telaye Fikadu

Instruction: Please oblige me by answering all questions by putting an **"x"** mark on your choice. Write your opinions on some of the questions you are requested. You do not need to write your name.

Part I: General information about the respondents

Name of the office_________________________________

Your position______________________________________

Sex Male ☐ Female ☐

Level of Education: BA/BSc degree and above ☐

Diploma (12+2) ☐ Grade 12 complete and certificate (12+1) ☐

Below Grade 12 ☐ Other (specify) ___________________

Years of job experience (total): 5 years and below ☐ 6-10 years ☐

11-15 years ☐ 16-20 years ☐ 21years and above ☐

For how long have you lived in this wereda? ______________________

Part II: Capacity building related issues

I. Human resource Development (Training)

1. Did you attend any training program since 2003?

Yes ☐ No ☐

1.1. If yes, (a) what type of training____

(b) For how long ____

1.2. If no, Why? State the reasons? ____

2. Would you please describe the topic of training you have participated in?

____

3. How do you evaluate the relevance of the training to the position you held and work engaged in?

Highly relevant ☐ evant ☐ So☐hat relevant ☐ Not relev☐ ☐

I do not know (specify) ______________________________

4. How often training programs are held in your organization?

Continuously ☐ y times ☐ Som☐es ☐ Rarely ☐ y rarely ☐ ☐

5. Would you rank the following in order of their participation in training programs in your office? Top officials ☐ le level managers ☐ Experts☐ Adminis☐e employees ☐

Others (specify) ____

6. Are training needs of employees, experts, and officials assessed before any training was undertaken?

Yes ☐ No☐do not k☐(why) ___________________________

7. If yes, are training programs conducted based on the assessed needs?

Yes ☐ No ☐ I do not ☐ (why) ___________________________

8. What are the basic capacity building challenges in your local government? __________

____

9. What solutions do you forward to tackle the problems? _____________________________

____

II. Management Capacity

How do you rate the capacity of your organization's managers?

No.	Management Capacity	High(3)	Satisfactory (2)	Low (1)
1	Building a shared vision and setting common goals for all employees			
2	Making decisions based on concrete evidences			
3	Making efforts to set standards, goals and objectives for performance			
4	Having communication skills			
5	Being cooperative			
6	Delegating authority and responsibility when appropriate			
7	Providing participatory decision making opportunities			
8	Making efforts to build the human capacity of the organization			
9	Having creativity and innovativeness			
10	Having knowledge of the current trends in organizational governance			
11	Having capacity to make acceptable organizational strategy			

III. Availability of Facilities

No.	**Items**	High(3)	Satisfactory (2)	Low (1)
1	Availability of telephone service			
2	Availability of vehicles			
3	Availability of computer service			
4	Availability of internet services			
5	Availability of computer networking			
6	Availability of strong database			
7	Availability of adequate buildings to support and facilitate daily work			

IV. Existence of Enabling Environment

No.	**Internal Environment**	High (3)	Satisfactory (2)	Low (1)
1	The existence of appropriate structure for key functions			
2	The existence of clear and stable structures and systems			
3	Employees' understand the objectives of the organization			
4	Line of authority is understood at all levels			
5	Availability of attractive work condition			
6	Availability of employee recognition programs (incentives, rewards, promotion) for high performance			

8. Key positions are adequately filled

A. Yes ☐ B. No ☐ C. Do not know ☐

9. The staff meetings are regularly held

A. Yes ☐ B. No ☐ C. Do not know ☐

10. Monitoring and evaluation capacity of the office is weak

A. Yes ☐ B. No ☐ C. Do not know ☐

11. State your reason for the above question? ____________________

12. The organization has clear rules, directives, and guidelines for employees

A. Yes ☐ B. No ☐ C. Do not know ☐

13. The financial management system of the office is weak

A. Yes ☐ B. No ☐ C. Do not know ☐

14. Explain your reason for any of your choice to the above question?____________________
____________________.

15. Plans are properly implemented in the office. A. Yes ☐ No ☐ do not know ☐

16. Would you please explain your reasons for any of your choice to the above question?
____________________.

External Environment

1. Do laws and procedures regarding powers and duties of woredas are clearly communicated except the constitution? A. Yes ☐ B. No ☐ C. Do not know ☐

2. Do Local level actors have clear visions over the goal of decentralization?

A. Yes ☐ B. No ☐ C. Do not know ☐

3. Does capacity building efforts enhanced the decentralization process in the locality?

A. Yes ☐ B. No ☐ C. Do not know ☐

4. Would you please explain your reasons for any of your choice to the above question?____

____.

5. Is the horizontal coordination in the local government weak?

A. Yes ☐ B. No ☐ C. Do not know ☐

6. Would you please explain your reasons for any of your choice to the above question?

____.

7. Do sectors/offices recognize and understand their current strength, weakness, opportunities and threats? A. Yes ☐ B. No ☐ C. Do not know ☐

8. Is the support from regional government sufficient?

A. Yes ☐ B. No ☐ C. Do not know ☐

9. Would you please explain your reasons for any of your choice to the above question?

____.

V. Community Participation

No.	**Community participation**	High (3)	Satisfactory(2)	Low (1)
1	Community participation in local development			
2	The local government administration makes regular meetings with the community			
3	The local communities are made to engage in planning and implementation of local development policies			
4	The existing development activities are given priorities of the community			
5	The local government is addressing the socio-economic problems of the local community			
6	The plans of the offices are communicated to the stake holders			
7	The office coordinates and communicate with the surrounding community			
8	The local government has a linkages with NGOs			
9	NGOs enter a contract or an agreement with woredas			
10	NGOs and donors consult woredas while planning			
11	Woredas consult NGOs and donors while planning			
12	The local government has a linkages with CBOs			

Annex 2

Addis Ababa University, School of Graduate Studies
Public Administration and Development Management

Capacity Building for Decentralized Local Governance: The case of Gindebebret and Abuna Gindeberet Wereda in Oromia National Regional State

Dear Respondents,

The aim of the research is to collect valuable information about the capacity of local governments, and capacity building efforts to the decentralization process and local governance in Gindeberet and Abuna Gindeberet Wereda under the title ***'Capacity Building for Decentralized Local Governance: The Case of Gindeberet and Abuna Gindeberet Weredas in Oromia National Regional State.'*** The data gathered from you will only be used for academic purpose, for M.A. thesis in Public Management and Policy, not for any other purpose. Therefore your definite data and answers are highly appreciated and will be kept confidential.

Thank you for your cooperation

Telaye Fikadu

Instruction: Please oblige me by answering all questions by putting an **"x"** mark on your choice. Write your opinions on some of the questions you are requested. You do not need to write your name.

Part I: General information about the respondents

Name of the office________________________________

Your position_____________________________________

Sex Male ☐ Female ☐

Level of Education: BA/BSc degree and above ☐

Diploma (12+2) ☐ Grade 12 complete and certificate (12+1) ☐

Below Grade 12 ☐ Other (specify) ____________________

Years of job experience (total): 5 years and below ☐ 6-10 years ☐

11-15 years ☐ 20 years 21years ☐ above ☐

For how long have you lived in this wereda? ______________________

Financial Capacity (To Financial Managers and Wereda officials)

No.	**Items**	High(3)	Satisfactory (2)	Low (1)
1	The discretion to set priorities and targets			
2	Ability to generate own revenue			
3	Diversified sources of revenue			
4	Expenditure decisions on the total amount of budget			
5	Budget is decided by regional governments in consultation with weredas.			
6	The budget is adequate to cover total recurrent and capital expenditures.			
7	Finances as provided in the budget are released timely.			
8	Awareness of the criteria used to apportion the budget (block grant)			
9	The formula enables appropriate allocation of resources			
10	Are you happy with the budget formula and the amount of money you get			
11	The adequacy of power and autonomy to decide on the block grant budget.			
12	The adequacy of available human resources to ensure a good financial control and information system			
13	The auditors of the organization are happy with the controls of cash and assets being utilized			

14. Are the previous grants been properly managed? A. Yes ☐ B. No ☐ C. Do not know ☐

15. Would you please explain your reasons for any of your choice to the above question? ____.

Annex-3

Interview Guide for key Informants

1. Does the organization have training and development policy, and budget for training and development and techniques to track these costs? Are there capacity building training programs being undertaken by your organization? If so, how are the focuses of the training identified? Is there training need assessment before the training program is thought to be organized? How are the trainees selected?
2. How do you evaluate the performance of officials and sectors in your locality? What does the capacity development efforts of the area look like? What does the human capacity of the locality look like?
3. Is there human development plans prepared for sectoral offices in the local government? What instruments are there to effect the plan? Is there a coordination mechanism at regional and local levels to ensure the implementation of the plan in all sectoral offices?
4. What does the participation of the community look like in matters that affect their life (Planning, implementation, monitoring, and evaluation)?
5. What important partnerships are established with NGOs and civil society groups in order to support the capacity building initiatives and local development?
6. Are there clear policies, guidelines, rules, and procedures to guide top level officials and employees?
7. Do sectoral offices have strategic plan? If so, is it subject to frequent revision to adapt it to changing circumstances? Do sectors or offices recognize and understand their (SWOT) strengths, weakness, opportunities and threats? Is the governing body active in acquiring and protecting core resources?
8. Is there clear line of accountability and communications among officials and employees in order to smooth the working conditions?
9. What are the basic socio-economic problems in the locality?
10. What are the obstacles that hinder the effective and efficient implementations of local government's mandate and responsibility? What do you think are the best solutions to deal with scapegoats to local government's activity?

Annex 4

Interview Guide for Focus Group Discussion

1. Does the organization have training and development policy, and budget for training and development and techniques to track these costs? Are there capacity building training programs being undertaken by your organization? If so, how are the focuses of the training identified? Is there training need assessment before the training program is thought to be organized? How are the trainees selected?
2. How do you evaluate the performance of officials and sectors in your locality? What does the capacity development efforts of the area look like? What does the human capacity of the locality look like?
3. Is there human development plans prepared for sectoral offices in the local government? What instruments are there to effect the plan? Is there a coordination mechanism at regional and local levels to ensure the implementation of the plan in all sectoral offices?
4. Are staff positions properly classified and allocated in adequate numbers to meet the standards for the accepted quality of service desired? Are position and duties clearly defined and communicated to employees?
5. Is there an organizational strategy? Is it generally accepted and supported in the organization? Has the strategy helped clarify priorities giving the organization a way to assess its performance? Is there a process for clarifying and revising the organization's mission and beliefs, for working on its goals, and for understanding its clients and users? Does it identify the opportunities and constraints regarding core resource areas?
6. Do sectors recognize their current strength, weakness, opportunity and threats?
7. How is the community participating in the development activities of your locality?
8. Does the local government have the discretion to set priorities and targets? How do you evaluate the ability of the local government to generate its own revenue and the adequacy to cover total recurrent and capital expenditures? Are there diversified sources of revenue? Does local government have adequate power and autonomy to decide on the block grant budget?

9. Are there adequate human resources to ensure a good financial control and information system? The auditors of the organization are happy with the controls of cash and assets being utilized
10. How do you evaluate the overall capacity of sectors and the local government as well as implementing agencies to address the socio-economic problems of the community?
11. How do you evaluate the commitment of the local leadership at addressing the socio-economic problems of the locality/the woreda?
12. How do you evaluate the extent of the participation of NGOs and CBOs in local development?
13. Is there clear line of accountability and communications among officials and employees in order to smooth the working conditions?
14. What are the basic socio-economic problems in the locality?
15. What are the obstacles that hinder the effective and efficient implementations of local government's mandate and responsibility? What do you think are the best solutions to deal with problems to local government's activity?
16. How do you evaluate the success or failure of capacity building program in this woreda? What are the changes observed in the woreda since the implementation of capacity building program? What are factors that contributed to the success or failures of the program?

Annex-5

MAP OF OROMIA NATIONAL REGIONAL STATE

Source: www.ethiodemographyandhealth.org

Annex - 6

Map of Abuna Gindeberet Woreda

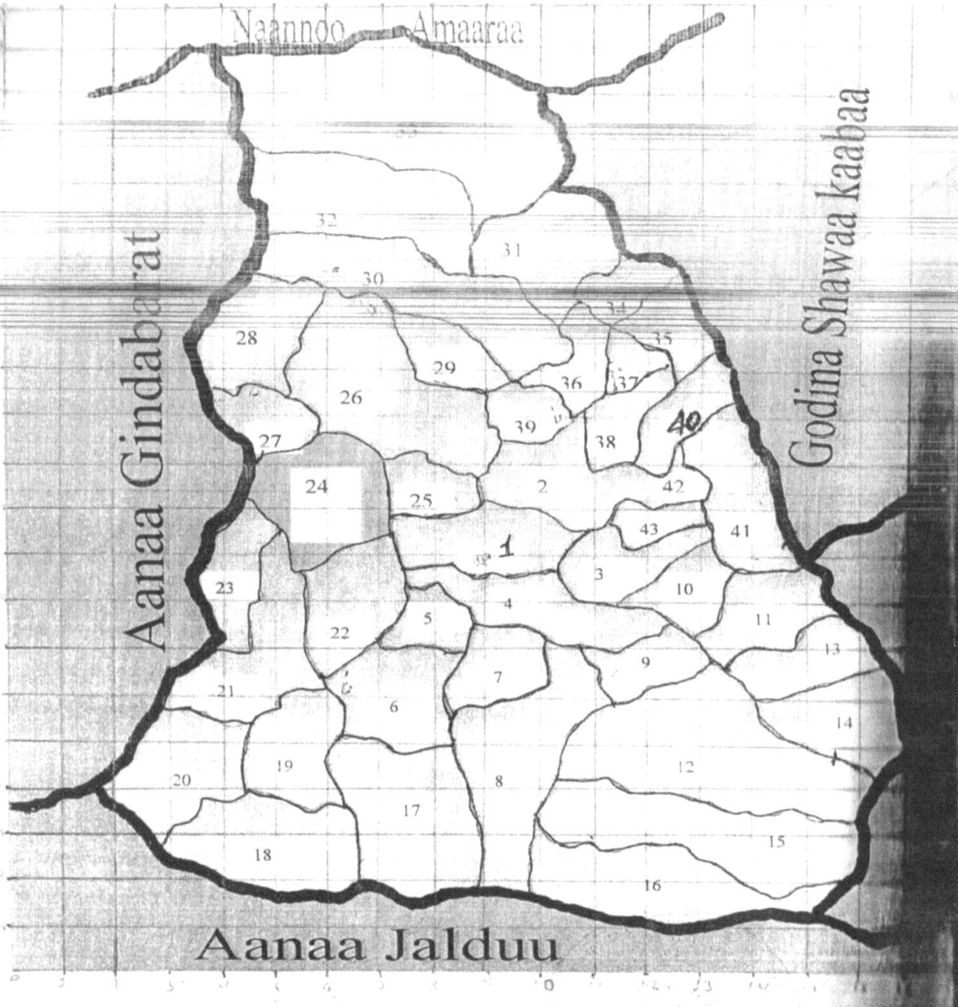

Source: Abuna Gindeberet Woreda office of Government Communication Affairs

Annex-7

Map of Gindeberet Woreda

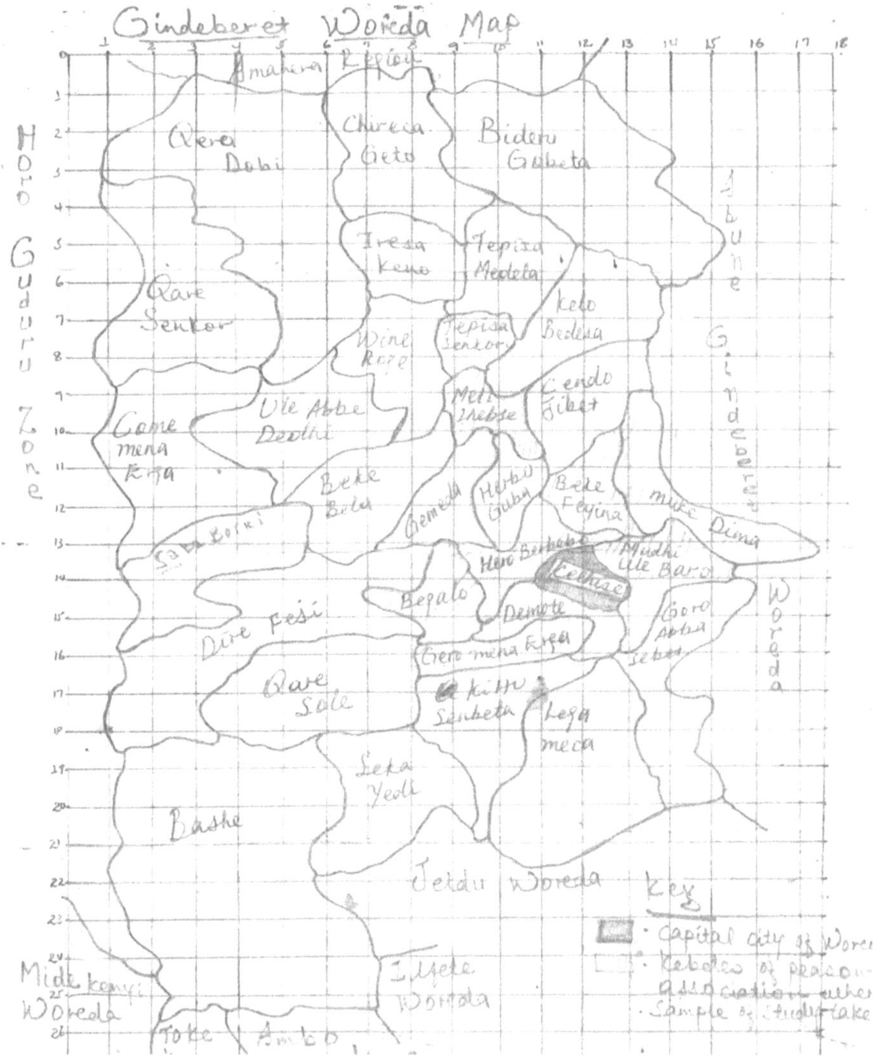

Source: Gindeberet Woreda office of Government Communication Affairs